MW00527020

Bosnian Vocabulary:
A Bosnian Language Guide

Dalila Kurjak

Contents

List of Bosnian letters

Order	Bosnian Latin alphabet	Bosnian Cyrillic alphabet	IPA
01	A a	А а	/ a /
02	B b	Б б	/ b /
03	C c	Ц ц	/ t͡s /
04	Č č	Ч ч	/ t͡ʃ /
05	Ć ć	Ћ ћ	/ t͡ɕ /
06	D d	Д д	/ д /
07	Dž dž	Џ џ	/ d͡ʒ /
08	Đ đ	Ђ ђ	/ d͡ʑ /
09	E e	Е е	/ e /
10	F f	Ф ф	/ f /
11	G g	Г г	/ g /
12	H h	Х х	/ h /
13	I i	И и	/ i /
14	J j	Ј ј	/ j /
15	K k	К к	/ k /
16	L l	Л л	/ l /
17	Lj lj	Љ љ	/ ʎ /
18	M m	М м	/ m /
19	N n	Н н	/ n /
20	Nj nj	Њ њ	/ ɲ /
21	O o	О о	/ o /
22	P p	П п	/ p /
23	R r	Р р	/ r /
24	S s	С с	/ s /
25	Š š	Ш ш	/ ʃ /

26	T t	Т т	/ t/
27	U u	У у	/ u/
28	V v	В в	/ ʋ/
29	Z z	З з	/ z/
30	Ž ž	Ж ж	/ ʒ/

1) Measurements
1) Mjere
1) Mjepe

acre

jutro

jутро

---

area

površina

површина

---

case

nonijus

нонијус

---

centimeter

centimetar

центиметар

---

cup

šoljica

шољица

---

dash

prstohvat

прстохват

---

degree

stepen

степен

depth

dubina

дубина

digit

cifra

цифра

dozen

tuce

туце

foot

stopa

стопа

gallon

galon

галон

gram

gram

грам

height

visina

висина

huge

ogromno

огромно

inch

inč

инч

kilometer

kilometar

километар

length

dužina

дужина

liter

litar

литар

little

malo

мало

measure

mjera

мјера

meter

metar

метар

mile

milja

миља

minute

minuta

минута

miniature

minijaturno

минијатурно

ounce

unca

унца

perimeter

perimetar

периметар

pint

pinta

пинта

pound

funta

фунта

quart

kvart, četvrtina galona

Кварт, четвртина галона

ruler
linijar
линијар

scale
skala
скала

small
malo
мало

tablespoon
kašika
кашика

teaspoon
čajna kašika
чајна кашика

ton
tona
тона

unit
jedinica
јединица

volume
volumen
волумен

weigh

vagati

вагати

---

weight

težina

тежина

---

width

širina

ширина

---

yard

jard

јард

Time
Vrijeme
Вријеме

What time is it?

Koliko je sati?

Колико је сати?

It's 1:00 AM/ PM

Trenutno je 1:00 sat

Тренутно је 1:00 сат

It's 2:00 AM/ PM

Trenutno su2:00 sata

Тренутно су2:00 сата

It's 3:00 AM/ PM
Trenutno su3:00 sata
Тренутно су3:00 сата

It's 4:00 AM/ PM
Trenutno su4:00 sata
Тренутно су 4:00 сата

It's 5:00 AM/ PM
Trenutno je 5:00 sati
Тренутно је 5:00 сати

It's 6:00 AM/ PM
Trenutno je 6:00 sati
Тренутно је 6:00 сати

It's 7:00 AM/ PM
Trenutno je 7:00 sati
Тренутно је 7:00 сати

It's 8:00 AM/ PM
Trenutno je 8:00 sati
Тренутно је 8:00 сати

It's 9:00 AM/ PM
Trenutno je 9:00 sati
Тренутно је 9:00 сати

It's 10: 00 AM/ PM
Trenutno je 10:00 sati
Тренутно је 10:00 сати

It's 11:00 AM/ PM

Trenutno je 11:00 sati

Тренутно је 11:00 сати

It's 12:00 AM/ PM

Trenutno je 12:00 sati

Тренутно је 12:00 сати

in the morning

ujutro

ујутро

in the afternoon

popodne

поподне

in the evening

navečer

навечер

at night

navečer

навечер

afternoon

popodne

поподне

annual

godišnje

годишње

calendar

kalendar

календар

daytime

dan

дан

decade

desetljeće

десетљеће

evening

veče

вече

hour

sat

сат

midnight

ponoć

поноћ

minute

minuta

минута

morning

jutro

јутро

month

mjesec

мјесец

night

noć

ноћ

nighttime

noć

ноћ

noon

podne

подне

now

sada

сада

o'clock

sati

сати

past

prošlost

прошлост

present

sadašnjost

садашњост

second

sekunda

секунда

sunrise

izlazak sunca

излазак сунца

sunset

zalazak sunca

залазак сунца

today

danas

данас

tonight

večeras

вечерас

tomorrow

sutra

сутра

watch

Ručni sat

Ручни сат

week

sedmica

седмица

year

godina

година

yesterday

jučer

јучер

Months of the Year

Mjeseci u godini

Мјесеци у години

January

Januar

Јануар

February

Februar

Фебруар

March

Mart

Март

April

April

Април

May

Maj

Мај

June
Juni
Јуни

July
Juli
Јули

August
 August
Аигуст

September
Septembar
Септембар

October
Oktobar
Октобар

November
Novembar
Новембар

December
Decembar
Децембар

Days of the Week
Dani u sedmici
Дани у седмици

Monday
Ponedjeljak
Понедјељак

Tuesday
Utorak
Уторак

Wednesday
Srijeda
Сриједа

Thursday
Četvrtak
Четвртак

Friday
Petak
Петак

Saturday
Subota
Субота

Sunday
Nedjelja
Недјеља

Seasons
Godišnja doba

Godišnja doba

Winter

Zima

Zima

Spring

Proljeće

Proljeće

Summer

Ljeto

Ljeto

Fall/ autumn

Jesen

Jesen

Numbers
Brojevi

Brojevi

One (1)

Jedan (1)

Jedan (1)

Two (2)

Dva (2)

Dva (2)

Three (3)

Tri (3)

Три (3)

Four (4)

Četiri (4)

Четири (4)

Five (5)

Pet (5)

Пет (5)

Six (6)

Šest (6)

Шест (6)

Seven (7)

Sedam (7)

Седам (7)

Eight (8)

Osam (8)

Осам (8)

Nine (9)

Devet (9)

Девет (9)

Ten (10)

Deset (10)

Десет (10)

Eleven (11)
Jedanaest (11)
Једанаест (11)

Twelve (12)
Dvanaest (12)
Дванаест (12)

Twenty (20)
Dvadeset (20)
Двадесет (20)

Fifty (50)
Pedeset (50)
Педесет (50)

Hundred (100)
Sto (100)
Сто (100)

Thousand (1000)
Hiljadu (1000)
Хиљаду (1000)

Ten Thousand (10 000)

Deset hiljada (10 000)
Десет хиљада (10 000)

One Hundred Thousand (100 000)
Sto hiljada (100 000)
Сто хиљада (100 000)

Million (1 000 000)
Milion (1 000 000)
Милион (1 000 000)

Oridinal numbers
Redni brojevi
Редни бројеви

first
prvi
први

second
drugi
други

third
treći
трећи

fourth
četvrti
четврти

fifth
peti
пети

sixth
šesti
шести

seventh

sedmi

седми

eighth

osmi

осми

ninth

deveti

девети

tenth

deseti

десети

eleventh

jedanaesti

једанаести

twelfth

dvanaesti

дванаести

thirteenth

trinaesti

тринаести

twentieth

dvadeseti

двадесети

twenty-first

dvadeset prvi

двадесет први

---

hundredth

stoti

стоти

---

thousandth

hiljaditi

хиљадити

---

millionth

milioniti

милионити

---

billionth

milijarditi

милијардити

Geometric Shapes
Geometrijski oblici
Геометријски облици

angle

ugao

угао

---

circle

krug

круг

---

cone

kupa

купа

cube

kocka

коцка

cylinder

cilindar

цилиндар

heart

srce

срце

heptagon

heptagon

хептагон

hexagon

heksagon

хексагон

line

linija

линија

octagon

oktagon

октагон

oval

oval

овал

parallel lines

paralelne linije

паралелне линије

pentagon

pentagon

пентагон

perpendicular lines

okomite linije

окомите линије

polygon

poligon

полигон

pyramid

piramida

пирамида

rectangle

pravougaonik

правоугаоник

rhombus

romb

ромб

square
kvadrat
квадрат

star
zvijezda
звијезда

trapezoid
trapez
трапез

triangle
trokut
трокут

vortex
vorteks
вортекс

Colors
Boje
Boje

beige
bež
беж

black
crna
црна

blue

plava

плава

brown

smeđa

смеђа

fuchsia

fuksija

фуксија

gray

siva

сива

green

zelena

зелена

indigo

indigo plava

Индиго плава

maroon

kestenjasta

кестењаста

navy blue

teget plava

тегет плава

orange

narandžasta

наранджаста

pink

roza

роза

purple

purpurna

пурпурна

red

crvena

црвена

silver

srebrna

сребрна

tan

žutomrka

жутомрка

teal

plavozelena

плавозелена

turquoise

tirkizna

тиркизна

violet

ljubičasta

љубичаста

white

bijela

бијела

yellow

žuta

жута

Related verbs
Povezani glagoli
Повезани глаголи

to add

dodati

додати

to change

promijeniti

промијенити

to check

provjeriti

провјерити

to color

obojiti

обојити

to count
izbrojati
избројати

to divide
podijeliti
подијелити

to figure
figurirati
фигурирати

to fill
ispuniti
испунити

to guess
pogoditi
погодити

to measure
mjeriti
мјерити

to multiply
pomnožiti
помножити

to subtract
oduzeti
одузети

to take

uzeti

узети

---

to tell time

reći vrijeme

рећи вријеме

---

to verify

verifikovati

верификовати

---

to watch

gledati

погледати

Michael is a **ten** year old boy who lives in Georgia. His family owns a **twenty acre** farm; he has **two** brothers and **three** sisters. Michael loves to work on his family's farm. He and his brothers wake up at **6:00 in the morning** every day. His favorite thing to do is ride his **brown** and **white** horse around the **perimeter** of the farm to check the fencing for damage. Even if there is only a **centimeter** of damaged wood, Michael must repair it. He also has to **measure** the **height** and **width** of the fence. He takes this job very seriously, so he doesn't want to miss a thing. Michael especially loves working on the farm in **autumn** because they sell more than **one thousand orange** pumpkins during the **month of October**! People from all over the state travel for **miles** to buy their pumpkins. Some of their pumpkins **weigh** as much as **one hundred pounds**! In the **winter**, his family sells Christmas trees. He loves helping other families find the perfect tree, whether it is **four feet, seven feet**, or even **nine feet tall**! In **December**, his family sells a **dozen green** trees a **day**, this keeps Michael very busy. In the **spring**, his family prepares the crops for the **summer** and **autumn** harvest. Because **spring** is such a busy time in school, each of the siblings take turns with special projects on the farm during the **week**; Michael's is the **first** day of the **week, Monday;** Henry's is the **second** day, **Tuesday;** Alan's is the **third** day, **Wednesday;** Sally's is the **fourth** day, **Thursday;** and Ann's is the **fifth** day, **Friday.** Little Ella is still too young for chores, but she loves to **measure** the **height** of the blooming **red** and **yellow** flowers with her **small ruler.** She is a **miniature** version of their mom. She cannot wait to grow up and help around the farm. During **summer,** Michael spends most of his **time** helping his mom cook. It is so hot outside, especially in **July** and **August;** he decided he needed a fun indoor activity. While cooking, he is learning how to **convert** different types of **measures,** like how many **teaspoons** are in a **tablespoon** and how many **cups** are in a **gallon;** he is also learning to add a **dash** here and sprinkle a **little** there to make the recipe just right. Mom knows cooking is a good skill to learn, but she also knows he will be learning these **measurements** in school this **September.**

Mihajl je **desetogodišnji** dječak koji živi u Džordžiji. Njegova porodica posjeduje farmu od **dvadeset jutara;** on ima **dva** brata i **tri** sestre. Mihajl voli raditi na farmi njegove porodice farmi. On i njegova braća se bude u **6:00 sati ujutro** svaki dan. On najviše voli da jaše svog **smeđe-bijelog** konja oko graničnog dijela farme kako bi provjerio da li je ograda oštećena. Čak i ako je samo **centimetar** oštećenog drveta, Mihajl to mora popraviti. On također mora **izmjeriti visinu i širinu** ograde. On shvata ovaj posao veoma ozbiljno, tako da ne želi ništa propustiti. Mihajl posebno voli raditi na farmi u **jesen**, jer tada prodaju više od **hiljadu naradžastih** bundeva tokom mjeseca **oktobra**. Ljudi iz čitave države putuju **miljama** kako bi kupili njihove bundeve. Neke od njihovih bundeva teže oko 100 **funti**! U **zimu** njegova porodica prodaje božićna drvca. On voli pomagati drugimporodicama da pronađu svoje savršeno drvce, bez obzira da li je ono **visoko četiristope, sedam stopa** ili čak **devet stopa**. U **decembru**, njegova porodica proda **desetak zelenih** drveća **dnevno**, time Mihajl bude vrlo zauzet. U **proljeće**, njegova porodica priprema usjeve za **ljeto** i **jesenju** žetvu. Zato što je **proljeće** naporno vrijeme u školi, svaki od braće i sestara se smjenjuju radeći na s posebnim projektima na farmi tokom **sedmice**; Mihajlov je **prvi dan u sedmici, ponedjeljak**; Henrijev je **drugi dan u sedmici, utorak**; Alanov je **treći dan u sedmici, srijeda**; Salin je **četvrti dan u sedmici, četvrtak**; i Anin je **peti dan u sedmici, petak**. Mala Ela je još uvijek premlada za poslove, ali ona voli **mjeriti visinu** cvjetajućih **crvenih i žutih** cvjetova svojim **malim linijarom**. Ona je **minijaturna** verzija njihove mame. Ona jedva čeka da odraste i pomaže oko farme. Tokom **ljeta**, Mihajl provodi većinu svog vremena pomažući mamioko kuhanja.Tako je vruće vani, posebno u **Julu i Avgustu**; on je odlučio da mu je potrebna zabavna aktivnost u zatvorenom prostoru. Dok kuha, on uči kako **konvertovati** različite vrste **mjera**, kao na primjer koliko je **čajnih kašika jedna kašika** i koliko **šoljica** je jedan **galon**; on također uči da dodaje **prstohvat** ovdje i posipa **malo** tamo da bi recept bio baš onako kako treba. Mama zna da je kuhanje dobra vještina za naučiti, ali ona također zna i da će ove **mjere** učiti u školi u **septembru** ove godine.

Михајл је **десетогодишњи** дјечак који живи уЏорџији. Његова породица посједује фарму од **двадесетјутара**; он има **два** брата и **три** сестре. Михајл воли радити на фарми његовепородице. Он и његова браћа се буде у **6:00 сати ујутро сваки дан**. Он највише воли да јаше свог **смеђе-бијелог** коња око граничног дијелафарме како би провјерио да ли је ограда оштећена. Чак и ако је само **центиметар** оштећеног дрвета, Михајл то мора поправити. Он такођер мора **измјерити висину** и **ширину** ограде. Он схвата овај посао веома озбиљно, тако да не жели ништа пропустити. Михајл посебно воли радити на фарми у **јесен**, јер тада продају више од **хиљаду нараджастих** бундева током **мјесеца октобра**. Људи из читаве државе путују **миљама** како би купили њихове бундеве. Неке од њихових бундева теже око **100 фунти**! У **зиму** његова породица продаје божићна дрвца. Он воли помагати другимпородицама да пронађу своје савршено дрвце, без обзира да ли је оно **високо четири стопе, седам стопа**или чак **девет стопа**. У **децембру**, његова породица прода **десетак зелених** дрвећа **дневно**, тиме Михајл буде врло заузет. У **прољеће**, његова породица припрема усјеве за **љето** и **јесењу** жетву. Зато што је **прољеће** напорновријеме у школи, сваки од браће и сестара се смјењују радећи на посебним пројектима на фарми током **седмице**; Михајлов је **први дан у седмици, понедјељак**; Хенријев је **други дан у седмици, уторак**; Аланов је **трећи дан у седмици, сриједа**; Салин је **четврти дан у седмици, четвртак**; и Анин је **пети дан у седмици, петак**. Мала Ела је још увијек премлада за послове, али она воли **мјерити висину** цвјетајућих **црвених и жутих** цвјетова својим **малим линијаром**. Она је **минијатурна** верзија њихове маме. Она једва чека да одрасте и помаже око фарме. Током **љета**, Михајл проводи већину свог времена помажући мами око кухања. Вани је вруће, посебно у **Јулу и Августу**; он је одлучио да му је потребна забавна активност у затвореном простору.. Док куха, он учи како конвертовати различите врсте **мјера**, као на примјер колико је **чајних кашика једна кашика** и колико **шољица** је један **галон**; он такођер учи да додаје **прстохват** овдје и посипа **мало** тамо да би рецепт биобаш онако како треба. Мама зна да је кухање добра вјештина занаучити, али она такођер зна и да ће ове **мјере** учити у школи у **септембру** ове године.

2) **Weather**
2) Vrijeme
2) Вријеме

air

zrak

зрак

air pollution

zagađenost zraka

загађеност зрака

atmosphere

atmosfera

атмосфера

avalanche

lavina

лавина

barometer

barometar

барометар

barometric pressure

pritisak zraka

притисак зрака

blizzard

mećava

мећава

breeze

povjetarac

повјетарац

climate

klima

клима

cloud

oblak

облак

cold

hladno

хладно

cold front

hladni vjetar

хладни вјетар

condensation

kondenzacija

кондензација

cool

svjež

свјеж

cyclone

ciklona

циклона

degree

stepen

степен

depression

depresija

депресија

dew

rosa

роса

dew point

temperatura kondenzacije

температура кондензације

downpour

pljusak

пљусак

drift

vodena struja

водена струја

drizzle

Sitna kiša

Ситна киша

drought

suša

суша

dry

suho

сухо

dust devil

pješčana vijavica

пјешчана вијавица

duststorm

pješčana oluja

пјешчана олуја

easterly wind

istočni vjetar

источни вјетар

evaporation

isparavanje

испаравање

eye of the storm

središte oluje

средиште олује

fair

vedro

ведро

fall
jesen
јесен

flash flood
bujica
бујица

flood
poplava
поплава

flood stage
stanje poplave
стање поплаве

flurries (snow)
sniježni naleti vjetra
сниједни налети вјетра

fog
magla
магла

forecast
prognoza
прогноза

freeze
ledeno
ледено

freezing rain

ledena kiša

ледена киша

front (cold/ hot)

fronta (hladna/ topla)

фронта (хладна/ топла)

frost

mraz

мраз

funnel cloud

tornado oblak

торнадо облак

global warming

globalno zagrijavanje

глобално загријавање

gust of wind

nalet vjetra

налет вјетра

hail

nepogoda

непогода

haze

izmaglica

измаглица

heat

vrućina

вручина

heat index

indeks topline

индекс топлине

heat wave

toplotni val

топлотни вал

high

visoko

високо

humid

vlažno

влажно

humidity

vlaga

влага

hurricane

uragan

ураган

ice

led

лед

ice crystals

ledeni kristali

ледени кристали

ice storm

ledena oluja

ледена олуја

icicle

ledenica

леденица

jet stream

protok vazduha

проток ваздуха

landfall

klizište

клизиште

lightning

munja

мунја

low

nisko

ниско

low pressure system

područje niskog pritiska

подручје ниског притиска

meteorologist

meteorolog

метеоролог

meteorology

meteorologija

метеорологија

microburst

dotok vazduha

доток ваздуха

mist

izmaglica

измаглица

moisture

vlaga

влага

monsoon

monsun

монсун

muggy

sparno

спарно

nor'easter

hladni prodor zraka

хладни продор зрака

normal

normalno

нормално

outlook

izgled

изглед

overcast

oblačno

облачно

ozone

ozon

озон

partly cloudy

djelimično oblačno

дјелимично облачно

polar

polarno

поларно

pollutant

zagađivač

загађивач

precipitation

oborine

оборине

pressure

pritisak

притисак

radar

radar

радар

radiation

radijacija

радијација

rain

kiša

киша

rainbow

duga

дуга

rain gauge

mjerenje količine padavina

мјерење количине падавина

relative humidity

relativna vlažnost

релативна влажност

sandstorm

pješčana oluja

пјешчана олуја

season

sezona

сезона

---

shower

pljusak

пљусак

---

sky

nebo

небо

---

sleet

susnježica

сусњежица

---

slush

bljuzgavica

бљузгавица

---

smog

smog

смог

---

smoke

dim

дим

---

snow

snijeg

снијег

---

snowfall

sniježne padavine

сниједене падавине

snowflake

pahuljica

пахуљица

snow flurry

nalet snijega

налет снијега

snow shower

sniježni pljusak

сниједни пљусак

snowstorm

sniježna oluja

сниједна олуја

spring

proljeće

прољеће

storm

oluja

олуја

storm surge

olujni val

олујни вал

stratosphere

stratosfera

стратосфера

---

summer

ljeto

љето

---

sunrise

izlazak sunca

излазак сунца

---

sunset

zalazak sunca

залазак сунца

---

supercell

grmljavinskaoluja

грмљавинскаолуја

---

surge

veliki talas

велики талас

---

swell

oteklina

отеклина

---

temperature

temperatura

температура

---

thaw

otopina

отопина

thermal

toplotno

топлотно

thermometer

toplomjer

топломјер

thunder

grom

гром

thunderstorm

grmljavina

грмљавина

tornado

tornado

торнадо

trace

trag

траг

tropical

tropski

тропски

tropical depression

tropska depresija

тропска депресија

tropical storm

tropska oluja

тропска олуја

turbulence

turbulencija

турбуленција

twister

vrtlog

вртлог

typhoon

tajfun

тајфун

unstable

nestabilno

нестабилно

visibility

vidljivost

видљивост

vortex

vorteks

вортекс

warm

toplo

топло

warning

upozorenje

упозорење

watch

motrenje

мотрење

weather

vrijeme

вријеме

weather pattern

obrazac vremenske prognoze

образац временске температуре

weather satellite

satelitska vremenska prognoza

сателитска временска прогноза

westerly wind

zapadni vjetar

западни вјетар

whirlwind

vihor

вихор

wind

vjetar

вјетар

wind chill

pad temperature

пад температуре

winter

zima

зима

Related verbs
Povezani glagoli
Повезани глаголи

to blow

puhati

пухати

to clear up

raščistiti

рашчистити

to cool down

osvježiti

освјежити

to drizzle

rominjati

ромињати

to feel

osjećati

ocjeħamu

to forecast

prognozirati

прогнозирати

to hail

padati

падати

to rain

kišiti

кишити

to report

izvjestiti

извјестити

to shine

sijati

сијати

to snow

sniježiti

сниježити

to storm

bijesniti

бијеснити

to warm up

zagrijati

загријати

---

to watch

posmatrati

посматрати

Heather loves the **seasons** and **weather**. She dreams of one day becoming a **meteorologist** so she can share her love with everyone. She is currently attending school to study the **weather** and how it works. She is learning that each of the four **seasons** brings its own **weather patterns** to the world. She is amazed at how the **seasons** affect the **weather**. The **seasons** vary throughout the world, but here in America, where Heather lives, there are four distinct **seasons,** and each of them brings something different to our world. In **winter**, the **temperature** is **cold** and the ground is white with **snow**. The **wind** gets so **cold** up on the mountaintop that the **wind chill** is below zero **degrees**. Sometimes, the **wind** blows with such force that it causes an **avalanche** of **snow** on the mountain. When the **air** is this **cold**, you are likely to wake up with **frost** on your car. In the **spring**, things begin to **heat** up. The **temperature** begins to **warm** up a bit, making the **snow** on the ground **thaw** out. The flowers begin to bloom and the trees begin to grow leaves. **Spring** often brings **rain**; sometimes the **rain** is so heavy, it causes **flash floods**. A common sighting in spring is a beautiful **rainbow** after the **rain**. The **temperature** is **hot** in the **summer**. The **temperatures** begin to rise and the **heat index** goes up causing a **heat wave**. There is not much **precipitation** in **summer**; however, occasionally the **clouds** bring a **thunderstorm**. The **rain** usually does not last long in **summer**, but the **thunder** and **lightning** can be dangerous. Every time there is a **thunderstorm**, Heather will watch the **weather report** to see if they will issue a **watch** or a **warning**. After **summer, fall** brings the start of **cool temperatures**. The leaves on the trees begin to fall, preparing the tree for the **winter**. In the coastal regions, **hurricanes** become a problem in the **fall**. This is a dangerous, yet exciting time in the world of **meteorology**. The **seasons** have a huge effect on **weather**; however the biggest changes in **weather** and the most dangerous events, such as **tsunamis, tornados,** and **storms**, occur during the change in **seasons**. The **unstable** and ever-changing **temperatures** affect the **barometric pressure** in a way that causes these types of events. While dangerous, they are exciting to someone like Heather who studies the **weather**. Heather's goal is to one day help educate and warn people in advance when these events are likely to occur.

Heder voli **godišnja doba** i **vrijeme**. Ona sanja da će jednog dana postati **meteorolog**, tako da može podijeliti svoju ljubav sa svima. Ona trenutno pohađaškolu za proučavanje **vremena** i kako onofunkcioniše. Ona uči da svako od četiri **godišnja doba** donosi svoje **vremenske obrasce**svijetu. Ona je zadivljena kako **godišnja doba** utiču na **vrijeme. Godišnja doba** se razlikuju širom svijeta, ali ovdje u Americi, gdje Heder živi, postoje četiri različita **godišnja doba** i svako od njih donosi nešto drugo našem svijetu. U **zimu, temperature** su **niske**i tlo je bijelo od**snijeg. Vjetar** postaje tako **hladan** na vrhovima planina da **temperatura opada** ispod nula **stepeni**. Ponekad, **vjetar** puše takvom jačinom da uzrokuje **lavinu snijega** na planinama. Kada je **zrak hladan**, vjerovatno ćete ujutro dočekati **mraz** na svom automobilu. U **proljeće** se stvari počinju **zagrijavati**. **Temperatura** počinje da se **zagrijava** pomalo, što **snijeg** na **tlu topi**. Cvjetovi počinju cvjetati i lišće na drveću počinje rasti. **Proljeće** često donosi **kišu**; ponekad je **kiša** toliko jakada uzrokuje **poplave**. Čest prizor u **proljeće** je lijepa **duga** nakon **kiše**. **Temperatura** je **visokaljeti**. **Temperature** počinju rasti i **indeks toplote** se povećava i uzrokuje **val vrućina**. Nema mnogo **padavina** u **ljeto**, međutim, povremeno **oblaci** donose **grmljavinu**. **Kiša** obično ne traje dugo, ali **munje i gromovi** mogu biti opasni. Svaki put kada dođe **grmljavina**, Heather će gledati **vremensku prognozu** kako bi vidjela da li će objaviti **motrenje** ili **upozorenje**. Nakon **ljeta**, **jesen** donosi početak **niskihtemperatura**. Lišće sa stabala počinje opadati, pripremajući drvo za **zimu**. U obalnim područjima, **uragani** postaju problem u **jesen**. To je opasno, ali uzbudljivo vrijeme u svijetu **meteorologije**. **Godišnja doba** imaju ogroman utjecaj na **vrijeme**, ipak najveće promjene u **vremenu** i najopasniji događaji, poput **cunamija, tornada** i **oluja**, pojavljuju se tokom promjena **godišnjih doba**. **Nestabilne** i stalno promjenjive **temperature** utiču na **pritisak zraka** uzrokujući ovakva dešavanja. Iako opasni, oni su i uzbudljivi za nekoga ko proučava **vrijeme poput Heder**. Hederin cilj je da jednog dana pomogne u edukaciji i upozori ljude unaprijed kada bi se ovi događaji trebali desiti.

Хедер воли **годишња доба** и **вријеме**. Она сања да ће једног дана постати **метеоролог**, тако да може подијелити своју љубав са свима. Она тренутно похађашколу за проучавање **времена** и како онофункционише. Она учи да свако од четири **годишња**

доба доноси своје **временске обрасце**свијету. Она је задивљена како **годишња доба** утичу на **вријеме**. **Годишња доба** се разликују широм свијета, али овдје у Америци, гдје Хедер живи, постоје четири различита **годишња доба** и свако од њих доноси нешто друго нашем свијету. У **зиму, температуре** су **ниске**и тло је бијело од**снијега**. Вјетар постаје тако **хладан** на врховима планина да **температура опада** испод нула **степени**. Понекад, **вјетар** пуше таквом јачином да узрокује **лавину снијега** на планинама. Када је **зрак хладан**, вјероватно ћете ујутро дочекати **мраз** на свом аутомобилу. У **прољеће** се ствари почињу **загријавати**. **Температура** почиње да се **загријава** помало, што **снијег** на тлу **топи**. Цвјетови почињу цвјетати и лишће на дрвећу почиње расти. **Прољеће** често доноси **кишу**; понекад је **киша** толико јака**да узрокује поплаве**. Чест призор у **прољеће** је лијепа **дуга** након **кише**. **Температура** је висока**љети**. **Температуре** почињу расти и **индекс топлоте** се повећава и узрокује **вал врућина**. Нема много **падавина** у **љето**, међутим, повремено **облаци** доносе **грмљавину**. **Киша** обично не траје дуго, али **муње и громови** могу бити опасни. Сваки пут када дође **грмљавина**, Хедер ће гледати **временску прогнозу** како би видјела да ли ће објавити **мотрење** или **упозорење**. Након љета, **јесен** доноси почетак ниских**температура**. Лишће са стабала почиње опадати, припремајући дрво за **зиму**. У обалним подручјима, **урагани** постају проблем у **јесен**. То је опасно, али узбудљиво вријеме у свијету **метеорологије**. **Годишња доба** имају огроман утјецај на **вријеме**, ипак највеће промјене у **времену** и најопаснији догађаји, попут **цунамија, торнада** и **олуја**, појављују се током промјена

годишњих доба. **Нестабилне** и стално промјењиве **температуре** утичу на **притисак зрака** узрокујући оваква дешавања. Иако опасни, они су и узбудљиви за некога ко студира **вријеме попут Хедер**. Хедерин циљ је да једног дана помогне у едукацији и упозори људе унапријед када би се ови догађаји требали десити.

3) People
3) Ljudi
3) Људи

athlete

atleta

атлета

---

baby

beba

беба

---

boy

dječak

дјечак

---

boyfriend

momak

момак

---

brother

brat

брат

---

brother-in-law

šogor

шогор

---

businessman

biznismen

бизнисмен

---

candidate

kandidat

кандидат

---

child/ children

dijete/ djeca

дијете/ дјеца

---

coach

trener

тренер

---

cousin

rođak

рођак

---

customer

mušterija

муштерија

---

daughter

kćerka

кћерка

---

daughter-in-law

snaha

снаха

---

driver
vozač
возач

family
porodica/ familija
породица/ фамилија

farmer
farmer
фармер

father/ dad
otac/ tata
отац/ тата

father-in-law
Svekar, punac
Свекар, пунац

female
žensko
женско

friend
prijatelj
пријатељ

girl
djevojčica
дјевојчица

girlfriend

djevojka

дјевојка

godparents

kumovi

кумови

grandchildren

unuci

унуци

granddaughter

unuka

унука

grandfather

deda

деда

grandmother

nana

нана

grandparents

nana i deda

нана и деда

grandson

unuk

унук

husband

muž

муж

instructor

instruktor

инструктор

kid

dijete

дијете

king

kralj

краљ

male

muško

мушко

man

muškarac

мушкарац

mother/ mom

majka/ mama

мајка/ мама

mother-in-law

Svekrva, punica

Свекрва, пуница

nephew

nećak

нећак

niece

nećakinja

нећакиња

parent

roditelj

родитељ

people

ljudi

људи

princess

princeza

принцеза

queen

kraljica

краљица

rock star

rock zvijezda

роцк звијезда

sister

sestra

сестра

sister-in-law
Jetrva, zaova, svastika
Јетрва, заова, свастика

son
sin
син

son-in-law
zet
зет

student
student
студент

teenager
tinejdžer
тинејџер

tourist
turist
турист

wife
supruga
супруга

woman
žena
жена

youth
omladina
омладина

Characteristics
Karakteristike
Карактеристике

attractive
Atraktivan, atraktivna
Атрактиван, атрактивна

bald
Ćelav, ćelava
Ћелав, ћелава

beard
brada
брада

beautiful
Lijep, lijepa
Лијеп, лијепа

black hair
crna kosa
црна коса

blind
Slijep, slijepa
Слијеп, слијепа

blond

plavuša

плавуша

blue eyes

plave oči

плаве очи

brown eyes

smeđe oči

смеђе очи

brown hair

smeđa kosa

смеђа коса

brunette

brineta

бринета

curly hair

kovrdžavakosa

коврджавакоса

dark

Taman, tamna

Таман, тамна

deaf

Gluh, gluha

Глух, глуха

divorced

Razveden, razvedena

Разведен, разведена

elderly

stariji

старији

fair (skin)

svjetla (koža)

свијетла (кожа)

fat

Debeo, debela

Дебео, дебела

gray hair

Sijed, sijeda

Сијед, сиједа

green eyes

zelene oči

зелене очи

handsome

Zgodan, zgodna

Згодан, згодна

hazel eyes

oči boje lješnjaka

очи боје љешњака

heavyset

krupne građe

крупне грађе

light brown

svijetlo smeđa

свијетло смеђа

long hair

duga kosa

дуга коса

married

udata/ oženjen

удата/ ожењен

mustache

brkovi

бркови

old

Star, stara

Стар, стара

olive

maslinast

маслинаст

overweight

Pretil, pretila

Претил, претила

pale
Blijed, blijeda
Блијед, блиједа

petite
mala
мала

plump
punačka
пуначка

pregnant
trudna
трудна

red head
crvenokosa
црвенокоса

short
Nizak, niska
Низак, ниска

short hair
kratka kosa
кратка коса

skinny
Mršav, mršava
Мршав, мршава

slim
Vitak, vitka
Витак, витка

stocky
Zdepast, zdepasta
Здепаст, здепаста

straight hair
ravna kosa
равна коса

tall
Visok, visoka
Висок, висока

tanned
Preplanuo, preplanula
Препלануо, препланула

thin
Mršav, mršava
Мршав, мршава

wavy hair
valovita kosa
валовита коса

well built
dobro građen
добро грађен

white

Bijel, bijela

Бијел, бијела

young

Mlad, mlada

Млад, млада

Stages of Life
Stadiji života

Стадији живота

adolescence

adolescencija

адолесценција

adult

odrastao

одрастао

anniversary

godišnjica

годишњица

birth

rođenje

рођење

death

smrt

смрт

divorce

razvod

развод

elderly

starost

старост

graduation

matura

матура

infant

malo dijete

мало дијете

marriage

brak

брак

middle aged

srednjih godina

средњих година

newborn

novorođenče

новориђенче

preschooler

predškolski učenik

предшколски ученик

preteen
dijete ispod trinaest godina
дијете испод тринаест година

senior citizen
penzioner
пензионер

teenager
tinejdžer
тинејџер

toddler
dijete koje je tek prohodalo
дијете које је тек проходало

tween
Blizanac, bliznakinja
Близанац/ близнакиња

young adult
mlada odrasla osoba
млада одрасла особа

youth
omladina
омлдина

Religion
Vjera
Bjepa

atheist
ateista
атеиста

agnostic
agnostik
агностик

buddhist
budista
будиста

christian
kršćanin
кршћанин

hindu
hinduista
хиндуиста

jewish
jevrej
јевреј

muslim
musliman
муслиман

sikh
sik
сик

Work
Posao
Посао

accountant
računovođa
рачуновођа

actor
glumac
глумац

associate
partner
партнер

astronaut
astronaut
астронаут

banker
bankar
банкар

butcher
mesar
месар

carpenter
stolar
столар

chef
šef
шеф

clerk
službenik
службеник

composer
kompozitor
композитор

custodian
Domar, čuvar
Домар, чувар

dentist
zubar
зубар

doctor
doktor
доктор

electrician
elektirčar
електирчар

executive

direktor

директор

farmer

farmer

фармер

fireman

vatrogasac

ватрогасац

handyman

majstor

мајстор

judge

sudija

судија

landscaper

vrtlar

вртлар

lawyer

advokat

адвокат

librarian

bibliotekar

библиотекар

manager

menadžer

менаджер

model

model

модел

notary

notar

нотар

nurse

medicinska sestra

медицинска сестра

optician

optičar

оптичар

pharmacist

farmaceut

фармацеут

pilot

pilot

пилот

policeman

policajac

полицајац

preacher

propovjednik

проповједник

president

predsjednik

предсједник

representative

predstavnik

представник

scientist

naučnik

научник

secretary

sekretar

секретар

singer

pjevač

пјевач

soldier

vojnik

војник

teacher

učitelj

учитељ

technician
tehničar
техничар

treasurer
rizničar
ризничар

writer
pisac
писац

zoologist
zoolog
зоолог

Related Verbs
Povezani glagoli
Повезани глаголи

to deliever
dostaviti
доставити

to enjoy
uživati
уживати

to grow
rasti
расти

to laugh

smijati se

смијати се

to love

voljeti

вољети

to make

praviti

правити

to manage

upravljati

управљати

to repair

popraviti

поправити

to serve

služiti

служити

to sing

pjevati

пјевати

to smile

smijati se

смијати се

to talk
pričati
причати

to think
razmišljati
размишљати

to work
raditi
радити

to work at
raditi u
радити у

to work for
raditi za
радити за

to work on
raditi na
радити на

to worship
obožavati
обожавати

to write
pisati
писати

John is a successful **pilot** and **businessman**. This came as no surprise to any of his **family** and **friends**, but his start in life wasn't an easy one. When he was just a **baby**, John spent a lot of time seeing **doctors** for a rare condition he was born with. As an **infant**, he was very sick and required the care of a **nurse** all the time. While he was in the hospital, everyone came to visit him; **aunts**, **uncles**, **cousins**, and of course his **grandparents**. Finally, he got well and he was able to live a normal, healthy life. Because of all he had been through, his **parents** knew he would be a successful **man**. As a **toddler**, he and his **grandfather** loved to watch planes fly over his house. John's **grandfather** told his **grandson** that he could be anything he wanted when he grew up. He was such a curious **child**, but never lost his love of planes, he even dreamed of being an **astronaut**. As he grew older, he really excelled in math and science class, his **teachers** were amazed and his **mom** and **dad** were so proud of him. He was the top **student** in his class when he graduated high school. He was a **tall**, **handsome young man** with **black hair** and **blue eyes**. He was also very talented on the basketball court; his **coach** thought he was a fine **youth** as well. He was just a **teenager** when he finished college and became a **pilot**, finally getting to live his lifelong dream. One day there was an accident that forced John into the hospital for quite some time, there he met a young **woman** named Rachel, and she was a **nurse**. John quickly recovered under the care of his **girlfriend**, but he was never able to fly again. He did however become a flight school **instructor** where he was able to teach other people how to fly. It wasn't long that John and Rachel because **husband** and **wife**. They had two lovely **children**, one **boy** and one **girl**. Jill is quite the **singer**; everything is a microphone to this aspiring

rock star. She is the cutest little **princess** you have ever seen! But Little Johnny Junior is following in his **father's** footsteps because he dreams of being a **pilot**, just like his **daddy**. **Father, son**, and **grandson** all love to spend quiet Sunday afternoons watching the planes go by. John knows that one day his **son** will be able to fly planes just like he did. While this thought scares him a little because of the accident, he is very proud of his **son** for his passion for flying. Maybe one day he will be a **student** in his **father's** flight school. In all of his successes, John's **family** is the achievement he is most proud of.

Džon je uspješan **pilot i biznismen**. To je postao bez iznenađenja bilo koga iz njegove **porodice i prijatelja,** ali njegov početak u životu nije bio lagan. Kad je bio **beba**, Džon je provodio dosta vremena posjećujući **doktore** zbog rijetke bolesti s kojom je rođen. Kao **malo dijete**, bio je veoma bolestan i bila mu je potrebna briga **medicinske sestre** sve vrijeme. Dok je bio u bolnici, svi su dolazili da ga posjete; **tetke, tetci, rođaci**, i naravno njegovi **dedo i nana**. Konačno, on je ozdravio i bio je u stanju da živi normalan, zdrav život. Zbog svega kroz šta je prošao, njegovi **roditelji** su znali da će biti uspješan **čovjek**. Kao **malodijete,** on i njegovi **dedo** su voljeli da gledaju avione dok lete iznad njegove kuće. Džonov **dedo** rekao je svom **unuku** da može biti sve sto želi da bude kad odraste. Bio je tako znatiželjno **dijete**, ali nikad nije izgubio svoju ljubav premaavionima, čak je sanjao da postane **astronaut**. Kakoje odrastao, briljirao je iz oblasti matematike i naukenjegovi **učitelji** su bili zadivljeni, a njegovi **mama i tata** su bili veoma ponosni na njega. Bio je najbolji **učenik**u svom razredu kad je **maturirao** u srednjoj školi. Bio je **visok, zgodan mladi muškarac s crnom kosom i plavim očima**. Bio je takođe veoma talentovan na košarkaškom terenu, njegov

trener je mislio da je bio fin **mladić**takođe. Bio je samo **tinejdžer** kad je završio koledž i postao **pilot**, konačno počinjući da živi svoj životni san. Jednog dana desila se nesreća koja je prisilila Džona u bolnicu na duževrijeme, tamo je sreo **mladu ženu** po imenuRejčel, i ona je bila **medicinska sestra**. Džon se brzo oporavio pod brigom njegove **djevojke**, ali nikad više nije bio u stanju da leti. On je, međutim, postao **instruktor** u školi letenja gdje je mogaoda uči druge ljude kako da lete. Nedugo zatimDžon i Rejčel su postali **muž i žena**. Dobili su dvoje divne **djece**, jednog **dječaka** i jedn**udjevojčicu**. Džil je dobra **pjevačica**; sve je mikrofon ovoj ambicioznojrok zvijezdi. Ona je najslađa **mala princeza** koju ste ikad vidjeli! Ali mali Džoni džunior je slijedio očeve stope zato što on sanja da postane **pilot**, bas kao i **tata**. **Otac, siniunuk** svi su voljeli da provode mirna nedjeljna popodneva gledajućiavione dok prolaze. Džon zna da će jednog dana njegov **sin** biti u mogućnosti da leti avionima baš kao što je i on. Dok ga ove misli malo plaše zbog nesreće, on je veoma ponosan na svog **sina** zbog njegove strasti za letenjem. Možda jednog dana on bude **student** u školi letenja njegovog **oca**. Odsvih njegovih uspjeha, Džonova **porodica** je dostignuće na koje je najviše ponosan.

Џон је успјешан **пилот и бизнисмен**. То је постао без изненађења било кога из његове **породице и пријатеља**, али његов почетак у животу није био лаган. Кад је био **беба**, Џон је проводио доста времена посјећујући **докторе** због ријетке болеси с којом је рођен. Као **мало дијете**, био је веома болестан и била му је потребна брига **медицинске сестре** све вријеме. Док је био у болници, сви су долазили да га посјете; **тетке, тетци, рођаци**, инаравно његови **дедо и нана**. Коначно, он је

87

оздравио и био је у стању да живи нормалан, здрав живот. Због свега кроз шта је прошао, његови **родитељи** су знали да ће бити **успјешан човјек.** Као **мало дијете**, он и његови **дедо и нана** су вољели да гледају авионе док лете изнад његове куће. Џонов **дедо** рекао је свом **унуку** да може бити све сто жели да буде кад **одрасте.** Био је тако знатижељно **дијете**, али никад није изгубио своју љубав премаавионима, чак је сањао да постане **астронаут.** Какоје одрастао, бриљирао је из области математике и науке, његови **учитељи** су били задивљени, ањегови **мама** и **тата** су били веома поносни на њега. Био је најбољи **ученик** у свом разреду кад је **матурирао** у средњој школи. Био је **висок, згодан млади мушкарац** с **црном косом и плавим очима.** Био је такођер веома **талентован** на кошаркашком терену, његов тренер је мислио да је био фин младићтакође. Био је само **тинејџер** кад је завршио коледж и постао **пилот**, коначно почињући да живи свој животни сан. Једног дана десила се несрећа која је присилила Џона у болницу на дужевријеме, тамо је срео **младу жену** по именуРејчел, и она је била **медицинска сестра.** Џон се брзо **опоравио** под бригом његове **дјевојке**, али никад више није био у стању да лети. Он је, међутим, постао **инструктор** у школи летења гдје је могаода учи друге **људе** како да лете. Недуго затим Џон и Рејчел су постали **муж и жена.** Добили су двоје **дивне дјеце**, једног **дјечака** и еднудјевојчицу. Џил је добра **пјевачица**; све је микрофон овој амбициознојрок звијезди. Он је најслађа **мала принцеза** коју сте икад видјели! Али мали Џони џуниор је слиједио очеве стопе зато што он сања да постане **пилот**, бас као и **тата. Отац, син и унук** сви су вољели да проводе мирна недјељна поподнева гледајућиавионе док пролазе. Џон зна да ће једног дана његов син бити у могућности да лети авионима баш као што је и он. Док га ове мисли мало плаше због несреће, он је веома поносан на свог сина због његове страсти премалетењу. Можда једног дана он буде **студент** у школи летења његовог оца. Одсвих његових успјеха, Џонова **породица**је достигнуће на које је највише поносан.

4) Parts of the body
4) Dijelovi tijela
4) Дијелови тијела

ankle
nožni zglob
ножни зглоб

arm
ruka
рука

back
leđa
леђа

beard
brada
брада

belly
stomak
стомак

blood
krv
крв

body

tijelo

тијело

bone

kost

кост

brain

mozak

мозак

breast

grudi

груди

buttocks

zadnjica

задњица

calf

list

лист

cheek

obraz

образ

chest

prsa

прса

chin

brada

брада

ear

uho

ухо

elbow

lakat

лакат

eye

oko

око

eyebrow

obrva

обрва

eyelash

trepavica

трепавица

face

lice

лице

finger

prst

прст

finger nail

nokat

нокат

fist

šaka

шака

flesh

meso

месо

foot/ feet

stopalo/ stopala

стопало/ стопала

forearm

podlaktica

подлактица

forehead

čelo

чело

hair

kosa

коса

hand

ruka

рука

head

glava

глава

heart

srce

срце

heel

peta

пета

hip

kuk

кук

jaw

vilica

вилица

knee

koljeno

кољено

leg

noga

нога

lips

usne

усне

moustache

brkovi

бркови

mouth

usta

уста

muscle

mišić

мишић

nail

nokat

нокат

neck

vrat

врат

nose

nos

нос

nostril

nozdrva

ноздрва

palm

dlan

длан

shin

cjevanica

цјеваница

shoulder

rame

раме

skin

koža

кожа

spine

kičma

кичма

stomach

stomak

стомак

teeth/ tooth

zub/ zubi

зуб/ зуби

thigh

bedro

бедро

throat

grlo

грло

thumb

palac

палац

toe

nožni prst

ножни прст

toenail

nožni nokat

ножни нокат

tongue

jezik

језик

underarm

pazuh

пазух

waist

struk

струк

wrist

ručni zglob

ручни зглоб

Related Verbs
Povezani glagoli
Povezani glagoli

to exercise
vježbati
вјежбати

to feel
osjetiti
осјетити

to hear
čuti
чути

to see
vidjeti
видјети

to smell
mirisati
мирисати

to taste
okusiti
окусити

to touch
dotaći
дотаћи

One day an alien crash landed on planet Earth. He was very confused and didn't know where he was. As he explored this undiscovered world, he happened along a little boy named David. David was eight years old and wasn't scared at all; after all, he knew there were aliens and he was happy to finally meet one. The alien had a large **head** and funny pointing **ears;** and he moved in a curious way with six **legs**! The alien was so confused when he saw the boy, so he asked David, "Why do you look so funny?" David laughed and told him all humans look like this. David has a good **heart** and wanted to make sure the alien was familiar with the people of Earth, so he told him all about how we use our body parts. "Let me tell you all about these funny parts", replied David. "On top of my body is my **head**; we have two **eyes** to see; two **ears** to hear; a **nose** to smell; and a **mouth** to talk and eat." The alien was surprised because he had all of these parts, but they looked much different. "Well then, " said the alien, "what are those things you are standing on and why are there only two of them? David said, "These are **legs**, we just put one in front of the other and it makes us walk or run." The alien was amazed that the human could walk with only two **legs,** after all, he had six **legs** and he needed them all to get around! "What are those things that are dangling off your upper **legs**?" asked the alien. "Oh, these? They are called **fingers** and they are attached to my **hands** and **arms**. Look! Aren't they neat? I can wiggle them, tickle with them, I even use them to pick things up. They really come in handy for lots of different things." The alien really wanted a set of those fingers, and then to find out there are **toes** on the end of the **legs**... wow! He just had to have some! The alien wanted to know more, so he continued, "What is that stuff sticking up on the top of your **head**?" David replied, "That is called **hair.** It grows really fast, even after I cut it off, it just grows back out!!

Adult humans have **hair** on other parts of their bodies; **legs, arms, face,** even their **toes**!" "Why don't you have **hair** on those parts?" asked the alien. David told him that he would not grow **hair** on those parts until he grows up. The alien was satisfied with David's explanation of the human body parts and decided it was time to return home. David was sad to see him go, but so excited to tell his friends all about his encounter with such a curious alien.

Jednog dana, vanzemaljac se srušiona Zemlju. Bio je jako zbunjen i nije znao gdje je. Dok je istraživao ovaj neotkriveni svijet, naišao je na dječaka koji se zove Dejvid. Dejvid je imao osam godina i nije bio ni malo preplašen. Uostalom, on je znao da postoje vanzemaljci i bio je sretan što je konačno upoznao jednog. Vanzemaljac je imao veliku **glavu** i smiješne zašiljene **uši**, i hodao je na neobičan način na šest **nogu**! Vanzemaljac je bio toliko zbunjen kada je vidio dječaka, pa je pitaoDejvida: "Zašto izgledaš tako smiješno?" Dejvid se nasmijao i rekao mu da svi ljudi izgledaju ovako. Dejvid ima dobro **srce** i samo je želio da se pobrineda vanzemaljac bude upoznat sa ljudima na Zemlji, pa mu je ispričaosve o tome kako mi koristimo naše **dijelove tijela**. "Dopusti da ti kažem sve o tim smiješnim dijelovima", odgovorio je Dejvid. "Na vrhu mog **tijela** je moja **glava,** imamo dva **oka** kako bismo **vidjeli**, dva **uha** da bismo **čuli, nos** kako bismomirisali i **usta** kako bismo pričali i jeli." Venzemaljac je bio iznenađen, jer je on imao sve te dijelove, ali su izgledali mnogo drugačije. "Pa onda, " reče vanzemaljac, "šta su te stvari na kojima stojiš i zašto imaš samo dvije?" Dejvid reče, "Ovo su **noge**, samo stavimojednu ispred druge i tako možemo hodati ili trčati". Vanzemaljac je bio zadivljentime da ljudi mogu hodati samo na dvije **noge**, naposlijetku, on je imao šest **nogu** i sve su mu bile potrebne dabi se kretao! "Šta je to što ti visi sa tvojih gornjih **nogu?**", upitao je vanzemaljac. "Oh, ovo? To se zove **prsti** i oni su zakačeni za moje **šake i ruke**. Vidi! Zar nisusuper? Mogu njima mrdati, škakiljati s njima, mogu ih čak koristiti i zapodizanje stvari. One su zaista korisne za dosta raznih stvari." Vanzemaljac je stvarno htio set tih **prstiju,** a onda je saznao da postoje **stopala** na kraju **nogu** ... vau! On je jednostavno morao da imaiste! Vanzemaljac je želio znati više, pa je nastavio, "Šta je ta stvar koja strši sa vrhatvoje **glave?**" Dejvid je odgovorio, "To se zove **kosa**. Ona **raste** vrlo brzo, čak i nakon što je odsiječem, jednostavno **naraste** ponovno!! **Odrasli** ljudi imaju **kosu** na drugim dijelovima tijela: **nogama, rukama, licu**, čak i nanožnim prstima!" "Zašto ti nemaš **kosu** na tim dijelovima?" pitao je vanzemaljac. Dejvid mu je rekao da njegova **kosa** neće narasti na tim dijelovima dok neporaste. Vanzemaljac je bio zadovoljan Davidovim objašnjenjem o dijelovima ljudskog tijela i odlučio je da je vrijeme za povratak kući. Dejvid je bio tužan gledajući ga kako odlazi, ali i jako uzbuđen da ispriča svojim drugovima sve o svom susretu sa tako radoznalim vanzemaljcem.

Једног дана, ванземаљац се срушио на Земљу. Био је јако збуњен и није знао гдје је. Док је истраживао овај неоткривени свијет, наишао је на дјечака који се зове Дејвид. Дејвид је имао осам година и није био ни мало преплашен. Уосталом, он је знао да постоје ванземаљци и био је сретан што је коначно упознао једног. Ванземаљац је имао велику **главу** и смијешне зашиљене**уши**, и ходао је на необичан начин на шест **ногу!** Ванземаљац је био толико збуњен када је видио дјечака, па је питао Дејвида: "Зашто изгледаш тако смијешно?" Дејвид се насмијао и рекао му да сви људи изгледају овако. Дејвид има добро

срце и само је желио да се побрине да ванземаљац буде упознат са људима на Земљи, па му је ispričaosve о томе како ми користимо наше **дијелове тијела**. "Допусти да ти кажем све о тим смијешним дијеловима", одговорио је Дејvid. "На врху мог **тијела** је моја **глава**, имамо два **ока** како бисмо **видјели**, два **уха** да бисмо **чули**, **нос** како бисмо **мирисали** и **уста** како бисмо причали и јели." Венземаљац је био изненађен, јер је он имао све те дијелове, али су изгледали много другачије. "Па онда, " рече ванземаљац, "шта су те ствари на којима стојиш и зашто имаш само двије?" Дејvid рече, "Ово су **ноге**, само stavimojednu испред друге и тако можемо ходати или трчати". Ванземаљац је био zadivljentime да људи могу ходати само на двије **ноге**, napoclijetku, он је имао шест **ногу** и све су му биле потребне dabi cekretao! "Шта је то што tiviси са твојих горњих **ногу**?", упитао је ванземаљац. "Ох, ово? То се зове **прсти** и они су закачени за моје шаке и **руке**. Види! Зар niсysuper? Могу њима мрдати, шкакиљати с њима, могу их чак користити заподизање ствари. Оне су заиста корисне за доста разних ствари." Ванземаљац је стварно хтио сет тих **прстију**, а онда је сазнао да постоје **стопала** на крају **ногу** ...вау! Он је једноставно морао да има исте! Ванземаљац је желио знати више, па је наставио, "Шта је та ствар која стрши са врха твоје **главе**?" Дејвид је одговорио, "То се зове **коса**. Она **расте** врло брзо, чак и након што је одсијечем, једноставно нарасте поново!! Одрасли људи имају **косу** на другим дијеловима тијела: **ногама, рукама, лицу**, чак и наножним прстима!" "Зашто ти немаш **косу** на тим дијеловима?" питао је ванземаљац. Дејвид му је рекао да његова **коса** неће **нарасти** на тим дијеловима док не порасте. Ванземаљац је био задовољан Дејвидовим објашњењем о дијеловима људског тијела и одлучио је да је вријеме за повратак кући. Дејвид је био тужан гледајући га како одлази, али и јако узбуђен да исприча својим друговима све о свом сусрету са тако радозналим ванземаљцем.

5) Animals
5) Životinje
5) Животиње

alligator

aligator

алигатор

---

anteater

mravojed

мравојед

---

antelope

antilopa

антилопа

---

ape

Čovjekoliki majmun

Човјеколики мајмун

---

armadillo

Armadilo/ Pasanac

Армадило/ пасанац

---

baboon

babun

бабун

bat
šišmiš
шишмиш

bear
medvjed
медвјед

beaver
dabar
дабар

bison
bizon
бизон

bobcat
ris
рис

camel
kamila
камила

caribou
sob
соб

cat
mačka
мачка

chameleon

kameleon

камелеон

cheetah

gepard

гепард

chipmunk

vjeverica

вјеверица

cougar

kuguar

кугуар

cow

krava

крава

coyote

kojot

којот

crocodile

krokodil

крокодил

deer

jelen

јелен

dinosaur

dinosaur

диносаур

dog

pas

пас

donkey

magarac

магарац

elephant

slon

слон

emu

emu

ему

ferret

omčica

омчица

fox

lisica

лисица

frog

žaba

жаба

gerbil

skočimiš

скочимиш

giraffe

žirafa

жирафа

goat

koza

коза

gorilla

gorila

горила

groundhog

mrmot

мрмот

guinea pig

zamorac

заморац

hamster

hrčak

хрчак

hedgehog

jež

јеж

hippopotamus

nilski konj

нилски коњ

horse

konj

коњ

iguana

iguana

игуана

kangaroo

kengur

кенгур

lemur

lemur

лемур

leopard

leopard

леопард

lion

lav

лав

lizard

gušter

гуштер

llama

lama

лама

---

meerkat

merkat

меркат

---

mouse/ mice

Miš/ miševi

Миш/ мишеви

---

mole

krtica

кртица

---

monkey

majmun

мајмун

---

moose

los

лос

---

mouse

miš

миш

---

otter

vidra

видра

---

panda

panda

панда

panther

pantera

пантера

pig

svinja

свиња

platypus

Čudnovati kljunaš

Чудновати кљунаш

polar bear

polarni medvjed

поларни медвјед

porcupine

dikobraz

дикобраз

rabbit

zec

зец

raccoon

rakun

ракун

rat

pacov

пацов

rhinoceros

nosorog

носорог

sheep

ovca

овца

skunk

tvor

твор

sloth

ljenjivac

љењивац

snake

zmija

змија

squirrel

vjeverica

вјеверица

tiger

tigar

тигар

toad

žaba krastača

жаба крастача

turtle

kornjača

корњача

walrus

morž

морж

warthog

bradavičasta svinja

брадавичаста свиња

weasel

lasica

ласица

wolf

vuk

вук

zebra

zebra

зебра

Birds
Ptice
Птице

canary
kanarinac
канаринац

chicken
kokoška
кокошка

crow
vrana
врана

dove
golubica
голубица

duck
patka
патка

eagle
orao
орао

falcon
sokol
сокол

flamingo

flamingo

фламинго

goose

guska

гуска

hawk

jastreb

јастреб

hummingbird

kolibri

колибри

ostrich

noj

нoj

owl

sova

сова

parrot

papagaj

папагај

peacock

paun

паун

pelican

pelikan

пеликан

pheasant

fazan

фазан

pigeon

golub

голуб

robin

crvendać

црвендаћ

rooster

pijetao

пијетао

sparrow

vrabac

врабац

swan

labud

лабуд

turkey

ćurka

ћурка

Water/ Ocean/ Beach
Voda/ Okean/ Plaža
Вода/ Океан/ Плажа

bass

grgeč

гргеч

---

catfish

som

сом

---

clam

školjka

шкољка

---

crab

rak

рак

---

goldfish

zlatna ribica

златна рибица

---

jellyfish

meduza

медуза

---

lobster

jastog

јастог

---

mussel

dagnja

дагња

oyster

ostriga

острига

salmon

losos

лосос

shark

ajkula

ајкула

trout

pastrmka

пастрмка

tuna

tuna

туна

whale

kit

кит

Insects
Insekti
Инсекти

ant

mrav

мрав

---

bee

pčela

пчела

---

beetle

tvrdokrilac

тврдокрилац

---

butterfly

leptir

лептир

---

cockroach

bubašvaba

бубашваба

---

dragonfly

vilin konjic

вилин коњиц

---

earthworm

kišna glista

кишна глиста

flea

buha

буха

fly

muha

муха

gnat

mušica

мушица

grasshopper

skakavac

скакавац

ladybug

bubamara

бубамара

moth

moljac

мољац

mosquito

komarac

комарац

spider

pauk

паук

wasp

osa

оса

Related Verbs
Povezani glagoli
Повезани глаголи

to eat

pojesti

појести

---

to bark

lajati

лајати

---

to chase

ganjati

гањати

---

to feed

nahraniti

нахранити

---

to hibernate

zimovati (hibernirati)

зимовати (хибернирати)

---

to hunt

loviti

ловити

to move

micati

мицати

to perch

Spustiti se

Спустити се

to prey

hvatati

молити

to run

trčati

трчати

to swim

plivati

пливати

to wag

mahati

махати

to walk

hodati

ходати

Sarah is a seven year old girl who loves to visit the zoo. Her mom takes her to the local zoo at least once a week to see her favorite animals. This is an account of her usual visit to the zoo: When they arrive, they must pass by the **flamingos** and boy do they smell! They are pretty to look at, but don't get too close! Sarah insists that they visit her favorite animal first, the **elephants**. She loves how big, yet gentle they are. They spend time watching the **elephants** move about their habitat and one time, she even got to see an **elephant** paint! Next, they visit the Birds' Nest exhibit. They have many different species of **birds** on display, including **sparrows**, **robins**, **peacocks**, **canaries**, **hummingbirds**, they even have an **eagle**! The **eagle** is so majestic; it is Sarah's favorite **bird**. Sometimes the **eagle**'s trainer will put on a show and Sarah just loves to see it spread its wings! After visiting the birds, Sarah likes to visit the mammal section of the zoo. They have **bears**, **tigers**, **lions**, **monkeys**, they even have **pandas**! One of the **pandas** had twin babies last year and Sarah has really enjoyed watching them grow up. After lunch, they visit the **reptile** house; there are lots of scaly looking animals there! The **alligators** are big and scary, but Sarah likes to watch from a distance. They also have **frogs** in lots of different colors; some are green, some are yellow and black, and some are blue! The best animals in the **reptile** house are the **snakes**. Some are stretched out long and some are coiled up taking a nap! They come in many different colors as well. Did you know that **snakes** eat **mice**? Sarah once got to see a **snake** eat its lunch, it was a little yucky to watch, but neat to see how a **snake** eats. After visiting the **reptiles**, Sarah and her mom go to see the **meerkats** and **warthogs**. They always make Sarah think of her favorite movie characters. The **meerkats** are silly little creatures and the **warthogs** just lay around in the mud all day! Sarah then goes to visit the tallest animal in the zoo, the **giraffe**. One day she even got to feed one! Its mouth is very weird to touch and it has a long tongue. One of the more popular sites at the zoo is the petting zoo. Sarah gets to brush the coat of **goats, sheep,** and even **pigs**! One last stop, to ride the train. While on the zoo train, Sarah gets to see lots of different animals, such as **kangaroos, ostriches, turtles,** and many more! Maybe one day, Sarah's mom can talk her into going to the aquarium instead of the zoo. Sarah would surely enjoy seeing **sharks, whales,** and **jellyfish**!

Sarah je sedmogodišnja djevojčica koja voli da posjećuje **zoološki vrt**. Njena mama je vodi u lokalni **zoološki vrt** najmanje jednom sedmično kako bi vidjela svoje omiljene **životinje**. Ovako izgleda njen uobičajniodlazak u zoološki vrt: Kada stignu, moraju proći pored **flamingosa** a kako oni samo smrde! Lijepi su zagledati, ali ne približavaj im se previše! Sarah inzistira da prvo posjete njenu omiljenu životinju, **slonove**. Ona ih voli jer su veliki, ali ipak nježni. One provode vrijeme gledajući slonove kako se kreću po svom staništu, ajednom je vidjela čak i slona kako crta! Slijedeće posjećujuptičija gnijezda. Oni imaju mnogo različitih vrsta **ptica** na izložbi, uključujući **vrapce, crvendaće, paunove, kanarince i kolibriće,** imaju čak i **orla**! **Orao** je tako veličanstven; to je najdraža **ptica** od Sarah. Ponekad **orlov** trener priredišou i Sarah volida vidi kako on širi svoja krila! Nakon posjete **pticama**, Sarah voli posjetiti odjel**sisavaca u zoološkom vrtu**. Imaju **medvjede, tigrove, lavove, majmune,** imaju čak i **pande**! Jedna od **pandi** je dobila blizance prošle godine i Sarah je stvarno uživala gledajući ih kako rastu. Nakon ručka posjećuju kuću **reptila**; tamo ima mnogo ljuskavih životinja! **Aligatori** su veliki i strašni, ali ih Sarah voli gledati iz daljine. Također imaju **žabe** u mnogo različitih boja; neke su zelene, neke žute i crne, a neke su plave!

Najbolje **životinje** u **reptilskoj** kući su **zmije**. Neke su ispružene koliko su duge, a neke su savijene i spavaju. Ima ih u mnogo različitih boja također. Znate li da **zmije** jedu **miševe**? Sarah je jednom vidjela **zmiju** kako jede svoj ručak, i to je bilo malo odvratno za gledati, ali i supervidjeti kako **zmija** jede. Nakon posjete **reptilima**, Sarah i njena majka idu pogledati merkatai **bradavičavu svinju**. Oni podsjećaju Sarah na njene omiljene filmske likove. **Merkati** su blesava bića i **bradavičave svinje** samo leže u blatu po čitav dan! Sarah potom ide posjetiti najvišu životinju u zoološkom vrtu - **žirafu**. Jednog dana je čak i hranila jednu. NJihova usta su veoma čudna na dodir i imaju dug jezik. Jedno od najpopularnijih mjesta **u zoološkom vrtu** je diou kome se može prići životinjama. Sarah tu može da četka **krzno koza, ovaca,** pa čak i **svinja**! Posljednja stanica, vožnja vozom. Dok se vozi zoološkim vozom, Sarah može vidjeti mnogo različitih **životinja,** poput **kengura, nojeva, kornjača** i mnogo drugih. Možda jednog dana Sarahina mama je nagovori da odu u **akvarij,** umjesto u **zoološki vrt.** Sarah bi sigurno uživala gledajući **ajkule, kitove i meduze!**

Сарах је седмогодишња дјевојчица која воли да посјећује **зоолошки врт**. Њена мама је води у локални зоолошки врт најмање једном седмично како би видјела своје омиљене животиње. Овако изгледа њен уобичајниодлазак у зоолошки врт: Када стигну, морају проћи поред **фламингоса** а како они само смрде! Лијепи су за гледати, али не приближавај им се превише! Сарах инзистира да прво посјете њену омиљену животињу, **слонове**. Она их воли јер су велики, али ипак њежни. Оне проводе вријеме гледајући **слонове** како се крећу по свом станишту, аједном је видјела чак и **слона** како црта!

Слиједеће посјећују птичија гнијезда. Они имају много различитих врста **птица** на изложби, укључујући **врапце, црвендаће, паунове, канаринце** и **колибриће**, имају чак и **орла**! **Орао** је тако величанствен; то је најдража **птица** од Сарах. Понекад **орлов** тренер приредишоу и Сарах волида види како он шири своја крила! Након посјете **птицама**, Сарах воли посјетити одјелсисаваца у зоолошком врту. Имају **медвједе, тигрове, лавове, мајмуне**, имају чак и **панде**! Једна од **панди** је добила близанце прошле године и Сарах је стварно уживала гледајући их како расту. Након ручка посјећују кућу **рептила**; тамо има много љускавих животиња! **Алигатори** су велики и страшни, али их Сарах воли гледати из даљине. Такођер имају **жабе** у много различитих боја; неке су зелене, неке жуте и црне, а неке су плаве! Најбоље животиње у **рептилској** кући су **змије**. Неке су испружене колико су дуге, а неке су савијене и спавају. Има их у много различитих боја такођер. Знате ли да **змије**једу **мишеве**? Сарах је једном видјела **змију** како једе свој ручак, и то је било мало одвратно за гледати, али и супервидјети како **змија** једе. Након посјете рептилима, Сарах и њена мајка иду погледати **меркатаи брадавичаву свињу**. Они подсјећају Сарах на њене омиљене филмске ликове. **Меркати**су блесава бића асамо леже у блату по читав дан! Сарах потом иде посјетити највишу животињу у зоолошком врту - **жирафу**. Једног дана је чак и хранила једну. Њихова уста су веома чудна на додир и имају дуг језик. Једно од најпопуларнијих мјеста у зоолошком врту је диоу коме се може прићи животињама. Сарах ту може да четка **крзно коза, оваца**, па чак и **свиња**! Посљедња станица, вожња возом. Док се вози зоолошким возом,

Сарах може видјети много различитих **животиња**, попут **кенгура, нојева, корњача** и много других. Можда једног дана Сарахина мама јенаговори да оду у аквариј, умјесто у зоолошки врт. Сарах би сигурно уживала гледајући **ајкуле, китове** и **медузе**!

6) Plants and trees
6) Biljke I drveće
6) Биљке и дрвеће

acacia

bagrem

багрем

acorn

žir

жир

annual

godišnje

годишње

apple tree

jabuka

јабука

bamboo

bambus

бамбус

bark

kora

кора

bean

grah

грах

berry

bobica

бобица

birch

breza

бреза

blossom

cvat

цват

branch

grana

грана

brush

četka

четка

bud

pupoljak

пупољак

bulb

lukovica

луковица

bush

grm

грм

cabbage

kupus

купус

cactus

kaktus

кактус

carnation

karanfil

каранфил

cedar

kedar

кедар

cherry tree

trešnja

трешња

chestnut

kesten

кестен

corn

kukuruz

кукуруз

cypress

čempres

чемпрес

deciduous

listopadan

листопадан

dogwood

sviba

свиба

eucalyptus

eukaliptus

еукалиптус

evergreen

zimzelen

зимзелен

fern

paprat

папрат

fertilizer

đubrivo

ђубриво

fir

jela

јела

flower
cvijet
цвијет

foliage
lišće
лишће

forest
šuma
шума

fruit
Voće/ plod
Воће/ плод

garden
bašta/ vrt
башта/ врт

gingko
ginko
гинко

grain
žitarice
житарице

grass
trava
трава

hay

sijeno

сијено

herb

ljekovita biljka

љековита биљка

hickory

hikori

хикори

ivy

bršljan

бршљан

juniper

smreka

смрека

kudzu

kudzu

кудзу

leaf/ leaves

list/ lišće

лист/ лишће

lettuce

zelena salata

зелена салата

lily

ljiljan

љиљан

magnolia

magnolija

магнолија

maple tree

javor

javor

moss

mahovina

маховина

nut

orah

орах

oak

hrast

храст

palm tree

palma

палма

pine cone

šišarika

шишарика

pine tree

bor

бор

plant

biljka

биљка

peach tree

breskva

бресква

pear tree

kruška

крушка

petal

latica

латица

poison ivy

otrovni bršljan

отровни бршљан

pollen

polen

полен

pumpkin

bundeva

бундева

root

korijen

коријен

roses

ruže

руже

sage

kadulja

кадуља

sap

biljni sok

биљни сок

seed

sjeme

сјеме

shrub

grm

грм

squash

buča

буча

soil

zemlja/ tlo

земља/ тло

stem

stabljika

стабљика

thorn

trn

трн

tree

drvo

дрво

trunk

deblo

дебло

vegetable

povrće

поврће

vine

Vinova loza

Винова лоза

weed

korov

коров

Related Verbs
Povezani glagoli
Повезани глаголи

to fertilize
gnojiti
гнојити

to gather
skupiti
скупити

to grow
izrasti
израсти

to harvest
požnjeti
пожњети

to pick
pokupiti
покупити

to plant
zasaditi
засадити

to plow
orati
орати

to rake

grabiti

грабити

---

to sow

sijati

сијати

---

to spray

prskati

прскати

---

to water

zaliti

залити

---

to weed

plijeviti

плијевити

Farmer Smith was a kind old man. He ran the local farm and orchard. One day, while out harvesting **corn**, a bird hobbled over and sat down beside him. Farmer Smith noticed the poor little bird had a broken wing, so he gathered up his supplies and cradled the bird in one of his baskets. The bird could not fly and was helpless, so Farmer Smith decided to nurse the bird back to good health. He used a small piece of **bark** to bandage the broken wing. Every day Farmer Smith would take the bird for a walk and they would rest against the **trunk** of an old **oak tree** at the edge of the property. The farmer loved to tell the bird all about the different **plants** on his farm. He told of the **pine trees** that lined his property.

These **trees** were perfect Christmas **trees**. He told of the **flowers** that grew wild near the lake, he explained how they started as a seed, and then grew into a bulb, then eventually into a beautiful **flower**. They were so colorful and vibrant; they remind the farmer of his wife. He would bring her **roses** every day for her to use on the dinner table. His wife was a wonderful cook, she could cook anything that the farmer grew; **squash, pumpkin, pears, apples, cabbage,** and many more. The way she used the **herbs** was like magic! The little bird loved to hear the stories about the farmer's wife, just hearing about her brought the bird comfort. One day, while the farmer was out **tilling** the **soil,** he heard a small sound approaching him; he turned around to see it was the little bird he had been caring for. She had learned to fly again! The farmer decided it was time for the bird to go live in the **forest** again. She was strong enough and prepared to survive on her own. It was a sad day, but the farmer took the bird into the **deciduous forest** and released her. One day, in early spring the farmer noticed a bird on his window sill. He couldn't believe his eyes, it was the same bird. He was so pleased to see the bird again, for it reminded him of his wife. Now, every spring, the bird comes to visit the farmer. He and the bird go to that old **oak tree** and Farmer Smith tells a new story about his wife. I don't know whatever happened to that bird, but it visited the farmer every year until the farmer passed away. It even visited his window sill at the hospital the year before he died. No one has ever seen it happen, but I know that the bird brings a single **rose** to Farmer Brown's resting site. Some may see the bird as a small, helpless creature, but for Farmer Smith, the bird helped to fill a void for his remaining years.

Farmer Smit je bio ljubazni starac. Vodio je lokalnu farmu i voćnjak. Jednog dana, dok je brao **kukuruz**, ptica je proletjela iznad i sjela pored njega. Farmer Smit je primijetio da jadna mala ptica ima slomljeno krilo, pa je skupio svu svoju opremu i stavio pticu u jednu od svojih košarica. Ptica nije mogla letjeti i bila je bespomoćna, pa je farmer Smith odlučio njegovatipticu i vratiti je u dobro zdravlje. Iskoristio je mali komad **kore** kako bi namjestio slomljeno krilo. Svaki dan, farmer Smit bi poveo pticu u šetnju i odmarali bi naslonjeni na **deblo starog hrasta** na rubuimanja. Farmer je volio govoriti ptici sve o različitim **biljkama** na svojoj farmi. Pričao joj je o **borovima**koji su okruživalinjegovu farmu. Ovo **drveće** jebilo savršeno za božićna **drvca**. Pričao je o **cvjetovima** koji su rasli divlje u blizini jezera, objašnjavao je kako je započelo kao sjeme, a onda preraslo ulukovicu, a na kraju u lijepi cvijet. Bili su tako šareni i jarkih boja; podsjećali su farmera na njegovu ženu. On bi joj donosio **ruže** svaki dan da ih stavi za stol. Njegova žena je bila divna kuharica, mogla je skuhati sve što je farmer uzgajao: **buču, bundevu, kruške, jabuke, kupus** i još mnogo toga. Način na koji je koristila bilje je bio poput magije! Mala ptica je voljela slušati priče ofarmerovoj ženi, sami pomen na nju bi opuštao pticu. Jednog dana, dok je farmer **obrađivao tlo**, čuo je mali zvuk koji mu sepribližava; on se okrenuo da pogleda, to je bila ptičica o kojoj se brinuo. Naučila je da leti ponovno! Farmer je odlučio da je vrijeme da ptica ponovo ode živjeti u **šumi**. Bila je dovoljno jaka i spremna da opstane sama. To je bio tužan dan, ali je farmer poveo pticu u **listopadnu šumu** i oslobodio je. Jednog dana, u rano proljeće, farmer je primjetio pticu na njegovoj prozorskoj dasci. Nije mogao vjerovati svojim očima, to je bila ista ptica. Bio je tako sretan da vidi pticu ponovno, jer ga je podsjetila na njegovu ženu. Sada, svakog proljeća, ptičica dolazi u posjet farmeru. On i ptica idu do onog **starog hrasta** i farmer Smit priča novu priču o svojoj ženi. Ne znam šta se desilo sa tom pticom, ali je posjećivala farmera svake godine dok farmer nije preminuo. Posjećivala je čak i njegov prozor u bolnici godinu dana prije nego je umro. Niko nikada to nije vidio, ali znam da ptica donosi jednu **ružu** na mjesto počinka farmera Brayna. Neki mogu vidjeti pticu kao malo i bespomoćno stvorenje, ali farmeru Smitu je ptica pomogla da popuni prazninu u njegovimzadnjim godinama.

Фармер Смит је био љубазни старац. Водио је локалну фарму и воћњак. Једног дана, док је брао **кукуруз**, птица је пролетјела изнад и сјела поред њега. Фармер Смитх је примијетио да јадна мала птица има сломљено крило, па је скупио сву своју опрему и ставио птицу у једну од својих кошарица. Птица није могла летјети и била је беспомоћна, па је фармер Смит одлучио његовати птицу и вратити је у добро здравље. Искористио је мали комад **коре** како би намјестио сломљено крило. Сваки дан, фармер Смит би повео птицу у шетњу и одмарали би наслоњени на **дебло старог храста** на рубуимања. Фармер је волио говорити птици све о различитим **биљкама** на својој фарми. Причао јој је о који су окруживалињегову фарму. Ово **дрвеће** је било савршено за божићна **дрвца**. Причао је о **цвјетовима** који су расли дивље у близини језера, објашњавао је како је започело као сјеме, а онда прерасло улуковицу, а на крају у лијепи цвијет. Били су тако шарени и јарких боја; подсјећале су фармера на његову жену. Он би јој доносио **руже** сваки дан да их стави за стол. Његова жена је била дивна кухарица, могла је скухати све што је фармер узгајао: **бучу, бундеву, крушке, јабуке, купус** и још много тога. Начин на који је користила биље је био попут магије! Мала птица је вољела слушати приче о фармеровој жени, сами помен на њу би опуштао птицу. Једног дана, док је фармер **обрађивао тло**, чуо је мали звук који му сеприближава; он се окренуо да погледа, то је била птичица о којој се бринуо. Научила је да лети поново! Фармер је одлучио да је вријеме да птица поново оде живјети у **шуми** . Била је довољно јака и спремна да опстане сама. То је био тужан дан, али је фармер повео птицу у **листопадну шуму** и ослободио је. Једног дана, у рано прољеће, фармер је примјетио птицу на његовој прозорској дасци. Није могао вјеровати својим очима, то је била иста птица. Био је тако сретан да види птицу поново, јер га је подсјетила на његову жену. Сада, сваког прољећа, птичица долази у посјет фармеру. Он и птица иду до оног **старог храста** и фармер Смитх прича нову причу о својој жени. Не знам шта се десило са том птицом, али је посјећивала фармера сваке године док фармер није преминуо. Посјећивала је чак и његов прозор у болници годину дана прије него је умро. Нико никада то није видио, али знам да птица доноси једну **ружу** на мјесто починка фармера Брауна. Неки могу видјети птицу као мало и беспомоћно створење, али фармеру Смиту је птица помогла да попуни празнину у његовим задњим годинама.

7) Meeting Each Other
7) Upoznavanje
7) Упознавање

Greetings/ Introductions:
Pozdravi/ Predstavljanje
Поздрави/ Представљање

Good morning
Dobro jutro   do-bro – you-tro
Добро јутро

Good afternoon
Dobar dan   do-bro dagun
Добар дан

Good evening
Dobro veče   vech-et
Добро вече

Good night
Laku noć   La-ka Noch
Лаку ноћ

Hi
Ćao   chow!
Ћао

Hello
Zdravo   Z-dravo
Здаво

Have you met (name)?

Da li ste upoznali (ime)?

Да ли сте упознали (име)?

Haven't we met?

Zar se nismo upoznali?

Зар се нисмо упознали?

How are you?

Kako ste?

Како сте?

stĕ-y

How are you today?

Kako ste danas?

Како сте данас?

How do you do?

Šta ima?

Шта има?

sh-tay-mah

How's it going?

Kako ide?

Како иде?

ka-ko E-day

I am (name)

Ja sam (ime)

Ja сам (име)

I don't think we've met.

Mislim da se nismo upoznali.

Мислим да се нисмо упознали.

It's nice to meet you.

Drago mi je da smo se upoznali.

Драго ми је да смо се упознали.

Meet (name)

Upoznati (ime)

Упознати (име)

My friends call me (nickname)

Prijatelji me zovu (nadimak)

Пријатељи ме зову (надимак)

My name is (name)

Moje ime je (ime)

Моје име је (име)

Nice to meet you.

Drago mi je da smo se upoznali.

Драго ми је да смо се упознали.

Nice to see you again.

Lijepo je vidjeti te opet.

Лијепо је видјети те опет.

Pleased to meet you.

Drago mi je da smo se upoznali.

Драго ми је да смо се упознали.

This is (name)

Ovo je (ime)

Ово је (име)

What's your name?

Kako se zoveš?

Како се зовеш?

Who are you?

Ko si ti?

Ко си ти?

Greeting Answers
Pozdravni odgovori
Поздравни одговори

Fine, thanks

Dobro, hvala

Добро, хвала

I'm exhausted

Iscrpljen sam

Исцрпљен сам

I'm okay

Dobro sam

Добро сам

I'm sick

Bolestan sam

Болестан сам

I'm tired

Umoran sam

Уморан сам

Not too bad

Nije loše

Није лоше

Not too well, actually

Nije baš dobro, zapravo

Није баш добро, заправо

Very well

Vrlo dobro

Врло добро

Saying Goodbye
Pozdravljanje pri odlasku

Поздрављање при одласку

Bye

Zdravo

Здраво

Good bye

Zbogom

Збогом

Good night

Laku noć

Лаку ноћ

See you

Vidimo se

Видимо се

See you later

Vidimo se poslije

Видимо се послије

See you next week

Vidimo se naredne sedmice

Видимо се наредне седмице

See you soon

Vidimo se uskoro

Видимо се ускоро

See you tomorrow

Vidimo se sutra

Видимо се сутра

Courtesy

Uljudnost

Уљудност

Excuse me

Izvinite

Извините

Pardon me

Pardon (izvinite)

Пардон (извините)

I'm sorry

Žao mi je

Жао ми је

Thanks
Hvala
Хвала

Thank you
Hvala vam
Хвала вам

You're welcome
Nema na čemu
Нема на чему

Special Greetings
Posebni pozdravi
Посебни поздрави

Congratulations
Čestitam
Честитам

Get well soon
Ozdravi brzo
Оздрави брзо

Good luck
Sretno
Сретно

Happy New Year
Sretna Nova godina
Сретна Нова година

Happy Easter

Sretan Uskrs

Сретан Ускрс

Merry Christmas

Čestit Božić

Честит Божић

Well done

Dobro urađeno

Добро урађено

Related Verbs

Povezani glagoli

Повезани глаголи

to greet

pozdraviti

поздравити

to meet

upoznati

упознати

to say

reći

рећи

to shake hands

Rukovati se

руковати се

to talk

pričati

причати

---

to thank

zahvaliti

захвалити

This is the story of a man named Pop. He just started a new job as a greeter at the local discount store. His son was so proud, he gave him a card that said, "**Congratulations**". He is a little nervous because he has never been a store greeter before. Throughout the day, there are so many customers going in and out of the store, sometimes Pop forgets what he should say. "**Pleased to meet you**" or "**Can I help you out?**" are good options for being polite. His manager assured him, saying, "You will be just fine, so don't worry." He begins the work day with a smile on his face, but by the end of the day, his smile is erased. "**Good morning,** " he says with a smile to the nice lady walking down the produce aisle. "**How are you doing?**" asked Pop, but she must not have heard him, because she didn't stop to say **hello.** "Hmm", said Pop, I guess she didn't hear me because a polite person would have said something like, '**Fine, how are you?**' or '**I'm fine, thank you.**' Next there was man with a bushy white beard, he looked very friendly and kind. Pop greeted him politely and said, "**Happy New Year!**" The man just grunted and went on his way, I guess he wasn't friendly after all. Pop replied, "**Have a good day**!" The next several customers were polite and spoke to him. Some of the customers said, "**How do you do?**" and one said, "**My name is Jim. What is your name?**" As the day went on, Pop got really tired and his **greetings** were losing not seeming as effective as earlier in the day. His manager was upset, but gave him another chance. He warned Pop that just saying "**Hi**" or "**Hello**" wasn't enough for the friendly environment our customers are used to. "If you want to make a good impression, you have to be polite. You can say something like, '**Merry Christmas**' or '**Good day to you, sir**', but please be nice to everyone you meet. Finally, as the end of the day was nearing, Pop was very happy to finally be able to say, "**Good night**." He went home without his smile, but said tomorrow is a new day and I will make sure to smile for everyone.

Ovo je priča o čovjeku koji se zvao Pop. On je upravo započeo novi posao kao pozdravljač u lokalnoj diskont prodavnici. Njegov sin je bio jako ponosan, dao mu je karticu na kojoj piše "**Čestitamo**". On je malo nervozan, jer nikada nije radio kao pozdravljač u prodavnici ranije. Tokom dana je tu mnogo kupaca koji izlaze i ulaze u prodavnicu, ponekad Pop zaboravi šta treba da kaže. "**Drago mi je da smo se upoznali**" ili "**Mogu li vam pomoći**?" su dobre opcije da bude pristojan. Njegov menadžer ga je uvjerio, rekavši "Bit ćeš dobro, ne brini." On počinje dan sa osmijehom na licu, ali krajem dana njegov osmijeh nestaje. "**Dobro jutro**", kaže sa osmijehom lijepoj dami koja prolazi kroz proizvodni prolaz. "**Kako ide**?" pita Pop, ali ga ona sigurno nije čula, jer nije stala da kaže **zdravo**. "Hmm", kaže Pop, vjerovatno me nije čula, jer bi pristojna osoba rekla nešto poput "**Dobro, kako si ti?**" ili "**Dobro sam, hvala**". Slijedeći je bio muškarac sa čupavom bijelom bradom, izgledao je veoma prijateljski iljubazno. Pop ga je pozdravio pristojno i rekao "**Sretna Nova Godina!**" Čovjek je samo progunđao i otišao svojim putem, izgleda da ipaknije bio prijateljski nastrojen. Pop je odgovorio "**Lijep dan vam želim!**" Slijedećih nekoliko kupaca je bilo pristojno i pričali su sa njim. Neki kupci su rekli **"Kako ide?"** i jedan je rekao, **"Moje ime je Džim. Kako se ti zoveš?"** Kako je dan prolazio, Pop je postao umoran i njegovo **pozdravljanje** se gubilo i nije bilo efektivno kao ranije tog dana. Njegov menadžer je bio uznemiren, ali mu je dao drugu šansu. Upozorio je Popa da **"Zdravo"** ili **"Ćao"** nije dovoljno prijateljsko okruženje na koje su naši kupci navikli. Ako želiš ostaviti dobar utisak, moraš biti pristojan. Možeš reći nešto poput **"Sretan Božić"** ili **"Dobar dan, gospodine"**, ali molim te, budi dobar prema svima koje sretneš. Napokon, kako se bližio kraj dana, Pop je bio jako sretan da napokon može reći **"Laku noć"**. Otišao je kući bez svog osmijeha, ali je rekao sutra je novi dan i sigurno ću se smijati svima.

Ово је прича о човјеку који се звао Поп. Он је управо започео нови посао као поздрављач у локалној дисконт продавници. Његов син је био јако поносан, дао му је картицу на којој пише **"Честитамо"**. Он је мало нервозан, јер никада није радио као поздрављач у продавници раније. Током дана је ту много купаца који излазе и улазе у продавницу, понекад Поп заборави шта треба да каже. **"Драго ми је да смо се упознали"** или **"Могу ли вам помоћи?"** су добре опције да буде пристојан. Његов менаџер га је увјерио, рекавши "Бит ћеш добро, не брини." Он почиње дан са осмијехом на лицу, али крајем дана његов осмијех нестаје. **"Добро јутро"**, каже са осмјехом лијепој дами која пролази кроз производни пролаз. **"Како иде?"** пита Поп, али га она сигурно није чула, јер није стала да каже **здраво**. "Хмм", каже Поп, вјероватно ме није чула, јер би пристојна особа рекла нешто попут **"Добро, како си ти?"** или **"Добро сам, хвала"**. Слиједећи је био мушкарац са чупавом бијелом брадом, изгледао је веома пријатељски иљубазно. Поп га је поздравио пристојно и рекао **"Сретна Нова Година!"** Човјек је само прогунђао и отишао својим путем, изгледа да ипак није био пријатељски настројен. Поп је одговорио **"Лијеп дан вам желим!"** Сљедећих неколико купаца је било пристојно и причали су са њим. Неки купци су рекли **"Како иде?"** и један је рекао, **"Моје име је Џим. Како се ти зовеш?"** Како је дан пролазио, Поп је постао уморан и његово поздрављање се губило и није било ефективно као раније тог дана. Његов менаџер је био узнемирен, али му је дао другу шансу. Упозорио је Попа да **"Здраво"** или **"Ћао"** није довољно пријатељско окружење на које су наши купци навикли. Ако желиш оставити добар утисак, мораш бити пристојан. Можеш рећи нешто попут **"Сретан Божић"** или **"Добар дан, господине"**, али молим те, буди добар према свима које сретнеш. Напокон, како се ближио крај дана, Поп је био јако сретан да напокон може рећи**"Лаку ноћ"**. Отишао је кући без свог осмијеха, али је рекао сутра је нови дан и сигурно ћу се смијати свима.

8) House
8) Kuća
8) Кућа

air conditioner

klima uređaj

клима уређај

appliances

aparati

апарати

attic

tavan

таван

awning

nadstrešnica

надстрешница

backyard

dvorište iza kuće

двор陷ште иза куће

balcony

balkon

балкон

basement

podrum

подрум

bathroom

kupatilo

купатило

bath tub

kada

када

bed

krevet

кревет

bedroom

spavaća soba

спаваћа соба

blanket

pokrivač

покривач

blender

miješalica

мијешалица

blinds

roletne

ролетне

bookshelf/ bookcase

polica za knjige

полица за књиге

bowl

zdjela

здјела

cabinet

ormar

ормар

carpet

tepih

тепих

carport

nadstrešnica

надстрешница

ceiling

plafon

плафон

cellar

podrum

подрум

chair

stolica

столица

chimney
dimnjak
димњак

clock
sat
сат

closet
plakar
плакар

computer
računar
рачунар

couch
kauč
кауч

counter
Šank, pult
Шанк, пулт

crib
dječiji krevetac
дјечији креветац

cupboard
kredenac
креденац

cup

šolja

шоља

---

curtain

zavjesa

завјеса

---

desk

pisaći sto

писаћи сто

---

dining room

trpezarija

трпезарија

---

dishes

suđe

суђе

---

dishwasher

mašina za pranje suđa

машина за прање суђа

---

door

vrata

врата

---

doorbell

zvono na vratima

звоно на вратима

---

doorknob

kvaka na vratima

квака на вратима

doorway

ulaz

улаз

drapes

zavjese

завјесе

drawer

ladica

ладица

driveway

prilaz

прилаз

dryer

sušilica

сушилица

duct

cijev

цијев

exterior

eksterijer

екстеријер

family room

porodična soba

породична соба

fan

ventilator

вентилатор

faucet

slavina

славина

fence

ograda

ограда

fireplace

kamin

камин

floor

pod

под

foundation

temelji

темељи

frame

okvir

оквир

freezer

zamrzivač

замрзивач

furnace

peć

пећ

furniture

namještaj

намјештај

garage

garaža

гаража

garden

bašta

башта

grill

roštilj

роштиљ

gutters

oluci

олуци

hall/ hallway

hodnik

ходник

hamper

korpa

корпа

heater

grijalica

гријалица

insulation

izolacija

изолација

jacuzzi tub

džakuzi

џакузи

key

ključ

кључ

kitchen

kuhinja

кухиња

ladder

merdevine

мердевине

lamp

lampa

лампа

landing

prizemlje

приземље

laundry

vešeraj

вешерај

lawn

travnjak

травњак

lawnmower

kosilica

косилица

library

biblioteka

библиотека

light

svjetlo

свјетло

linen closet

ormar za posteljinu

ормар за постељину

living room

dnevni boravak

дневни боравак

lock
brava
брава

loft
potkrovlje
поткровље

mailbox
poštansko sanduče
поштанско сандуче

mantle
kamin
камин

master bedroom
glavna spavaća soba
главна спаваћа соба

microwave
mikrovalna
микровална

mirror
ogledalo
огледало

neighborhood
komšiluk
комшилук

nightstand

Noćni ormarić

Ноћни ормарић

office

ured

уред

oven

rerna

рерна

painting

slika

слика

paneling

tapete

тапете

pantry

špajz

шпајз

patio

dvorište

дворриште

picnic table

piknik sto

пикник сто

picture
fotografija
фотографија

picture frame
okvir za fotografiju
оквир за фотографија

pillow
jastuk
јастук

plates
tanjiri
тањири

plumbing
Vodovodne cijevi
Водоводне цијеви

pool
bazen
базен

porch
veranda
веранда

queen bed
bračni krevet
брачни кревет

quilt

jorgan

јорган

railing

ograda

ограда

range

šporet

шпорет

refrigerator

frižider

фрижидер

remote control

daljinski upravljač

даљински управљач

roof

krov

кров

room

soba

соба

rug

ćilim

ћилим

screen door

kliznavrata

клизнаврата

shed

šupa

шупа

shelf/ shelves

Polica/ police

Полица/ полице

shingle

šindra

шиндра

shower

tuš kabina

туш кабина

shutters

žaluzine

жалузине

siding

Drvena fasada

Дрвена фасада

sink

sudoper

судопер

sofa

sofa

софа

---

stairs/ staircase

stepenište

степениште

---

step

stepenica

степеница

---

stoop

stepenice

степенице

---

stove

peć

пећ

---

study

radna soba

радна соба

---

table

sto

сто

---

telephone

telefon

телефон

---

television

televizija

телевизија

toaster

toster

тостер

toilet

zahod

заход

towel

peškir

пешкир

trash can

kanta za smeće

канта за смеће

trim

drvenarija

дрвенарија

upstairs

na gornjem spratu

на горњем спрату

utility room

ostava

остава

vacuum

usisivač

усисивач

vanity

stol za šminkanje

стол за шминкање

vase

vaza

ваза

vent

ventilacija

вентилација

wall

zid

зид

wardrobe

garderober

гардеробер

washer/ washing machine

mašina za pranje veša

машина за прање веша

waste basket

kanta za otpatke

канта за отпатке

water heater

bojler

бојлер

welcome mat

otirač

отирач

window

prozor

прозор

window pane

prozorsko okno

прозорско окно

window sill

Prozorska daska

Прозорска даска

yard

dvorište

дворište

Related Verbs
Povezani glagoli
Повезани глаголи

to build

graditi

градити

to buy

kupiti

купити

to clean

čistiti

чистити

to decorate

urediti

уредити

to leave

napustiti

напустити

to move in

useliti

уселити

to move out

odseliti

одселити

to renovate

renovirati

реновирати

to repair

popraviti

поправити

to sell

prodati

продати

---

to show

pokazati

показати

---

to view

vidjeti

видјети

---

to visit

posjetiti

посјетити

---

to work

raditi

радити

Mike and Linda just bought their first **house**. It is a not a large house, but it is very cozy. It is in a very nice **neighborhood** and has a cute, well-manicured **lawn**. It has a small front **porch**, which will be nice to relax on in the evenings after work. The **exterior** is light blue with a dark blue **door** and **shutters**. It has a nice size **garage** that is big enough for both of their cars and a small **shed** out back for their lawnmower. The **backyard** is small, but has a cute little swing set. One day, maybe they will have kids to enjoy it. The **living room** is very spacious and is beautifully decorated in greens and blues. The **walls** are painted light blue and the **curtains** are patterned green and blue. The **couch** and **chair** are very comfortable and roomy enough for the few guests they may have on occasion. Mike is very excited about the new **television** they had installed on the **wall** above the **fireplace**. The **kitchen** is small, yet functional. It has a **refrigerator**, a **dishwasher,** an **oven**, and a built-in **microwave.** There is not much storage, so Linda will have to be very organized. The **walls** are painted yellow and it has a nice floral border. Linda did not pick it out, but it suits her taste well. The **house** has three **bedrooms**, which gives their family room to grow. The **master bedroom** is big enough to fit their **queen bed**, two **nightstands**, and a **dresser**. Linda has already picked out **curtains** to match the bedding. The **walls** are painted beige, but Linda thinks she can brighten the **room** with other decor. Linda's favorite part of the house is the master **bathroom**; it has a jacuzzi **tub** and she can't wait to try it out. It also has a separate **shower** and a double **vanity**. Mike works from home, so he plans to use one of the other, even smaller **bedrooms** as a home **office**. There is not a lot of space, but enough for his **desk**, **computer**, and a **bookshelf**. The back **porch** is nice and has a charcoal **grill** and a **picnic table.** Mike loves to cook on the **grill**, so it will be put to good use. They will need to get a **washing machine** and **dryer** for the **laundry room,** it is small, but it has a **sink**, which is very helpful when washing clothes. Overall, Mike and Linda picked out an excellent first home. It fits their budget, as well as their taste perfectly!

Majk i Linda su upravo kupili njihovu prvu **kuću.** To nije velika kuća, ali je veoma udobna. Nalazi se u veoma lijepom **komšiluku** i ima slatki, dobro njegovani **travnjak.** Ima malu prednju**verandu**, koja će biti dobraza opuštanje u večerima poslije posla. **Eksterijer** je svijetlo plav s tamno plavim **vratima** i **žaluzinama**. Ima **garažu** dobre veličine koja je dovoljno velika za oba njihova auta i ima malu **šupu** iza za njihovu **kosilicu**. **Dvorište** iza kuće je malo, ali ima slatku malu ljuljačku. Jednog dana možda budu imali djecu da uživaju na njoj. **Dnevni boravak** je veoma prostran i lijepo uređen zelenim i plavim bojama. **Zidovi** su ofarbani svijetlo plavom bojom, a na **zavjesama** su uzorci zelene i plave boje. **Kauč** i **stolica** su veoma udobni i prostrani dovoljno za nekoliko gostiju koje budu ponekada imali. Majk je veoma uzbuđen radi nove **televizije** koju su instalirali na **zidu** iznad **kamina**. **Kuhinja** je mala, ali funkcionalna. Ima **frižider, mašinu za pranje suđa, rernu** i ugrađenu **mikrovalnu**. Tu nema puno prostora, zato će Linda morati biti dobro organizovana. **Zidovi** su ofarbani žutom bojom i ima lijepu cvijetnu ivicu. Linda je nije odabrala, ali odgovara dobro njenom ukusu. **Kuća** ima tri **spavaće sobe**, što daje njihovoj porodici mjesta da raste. **Glavna spavaća soba** je dovoljna velika za njihov **bračni krevet**, dva **noćna ormarića** i **garderober**. Linda je već izabrala **zavjese** koje se slažu s posteljinom. **Zidovi** su ofarbani bež bojom, a Linda misli da može osvježiti **sobu** drugim dekoracijama. Lindin omiljeni dio kuće je **glavno kupatilo** koje ima **džakuzi kadu** i jedva čeka da je isproba. Također ima **odvojeni tuš** i **dupli stol za šminkanje**. Majk radi od kuće, pa planira da koristi jednu od manjih **spavaćih soba** kao **kućni ured**. Tu nema puno prostora, ali ima dovoljno za njegov **stol, kompjuter i police za knjige**. Stražnji trijem je lijep i ima **ugljani roštilj** i **piknik stol**. Majk voli da **roštilja**, zato će biti dobro iskorišteni. Morati će nabaviti **mašinu za pranje veša** i **sušilicu** za **vešeraj**, koji je mali, ali ima **sudoper** koji je koristan kada se pere odjeća. Cjelokupno, Majk i Linda su izabrali odličan prvi dom. Uklapa se u njihov budžet, kao i u njihov ukus perfektno!

Мајк и Линда су управо купили њихову прву **кућу**. То није велика кућа, али је веома удобна. Налази се у веома лијепом **комшилуку** и има слатки, добро његовани **травњак**. Има малу предњу**веранду**, која ће бити добра за опуштање у вечерима послије посла. **Екстеријер** је свијетло плав с тамно плавим **вратима** и **жалузинама**. Има **гаражу** добре величине која је довољно велика за оба њихова аута и има малу **шупу** иза за њихову **косилицу**. **Двориште** иза куће је мало, али има слатку малу љуљачку. Једног дана можда буду имали дјецу да уживају на њој. **Дневни боравак** је веома простран и лијепо уређен зеленим и плавим бојама. **Зидови** су офарбани свијетло плавом бојом, а на **завјесама** су узорци зелене и плаве боје. **Кауч** и **столица** су веома удобни и пространи довољно за неколико гостију које буду понекада имали. Мајк је веома узбуђен ради нове **телевизије** коју су инсталирали на **зиду** изнад **камина**. **Кухиња** је мала, али функционална. Има **фрижидер, машину за прање суђа, рерну** и уграђену **микровалну**. Ту нема пуно простора, зато ће Линда морати бити добро организована. **Зидови** су офарбани жутом бојом и има лијепу цвијетну ивицу. Линда је није одабрала, али добро одговара њеном укусу. **Кућа** има три **спаваће собе**, што даје њиховој породици мјеста да расте. **Главна спаваћа соба** је довољна велика за њихов **брачни кревет**, два **ноћна ормарића** и **гардеробер**. Линда је већ **изабрала** завјесе које се слажу с постељином. **Зидови** су офарбани беж бојом, а Линда мисли да може освјежити собу другим декорацијама. Линдин омиљени дио куће је **главно купатило** које има **џакузи каду** и једва чека да је испроба. Такођер има **одвојени туш** и **дупли стол за шминкање**. Мајк ради од куће, па планира да користи једну од мањих **спаваћих соба** као **кућни уред**. Ту нема пуно простора, али има довољно за **његов стол, компјутер и полице за књиге**. Стражњи **тријем** је лијеп и има **угљани роштиљ** и **пикник стол**. Мајк воли да **роштиља**, зато ће бити добро искориштени. Морати ће набавити **машину за прање веша** и **сушилицу** за **вешерај**, који је мали, али има **судопер** који је користан када се пере одјећа. Цјелокупно, Мајк и Линда су изабрали одличан први дом. Уклапа се у њихов буџет, као и у њихов укус перфектно!

9) Arts & Entertainment
9) Umjetnost i zabava
9) Умјетност и забава

3-D

3-D

3-Д

action movie

akcioni film

акциони филм

actor/ actress

glumac/ glumica

глумац/ глумица

album

album

албум

alternative

alternativa

алтернатива

amphitheater

amfiteatar

амфитеатар

animation

animacija

анимација

artist

umjetnik

умјетник

audience

publika

публика

ballerina

balerina

балерина

ballet

balet

балет

band

bend

бенд

blues

bluz

блуз

caption

naslov

наслов

carnival

karneval

карневал

cast

glumačka ekipa

глумачка екипа

choreographer

koreograf

кореограф

cinema

kino

кино

classic

klasik

класик

comedy

komedija

комедија

commercial

komercijalno

комерцијално

composer

kompozitor

композитор

concert

koncert

концерт

conductor

dirigent

диригент

contemporary

savremen

савремен

country

zemlja

земља

credits

zasluge

заслуге

dancer

plesač

плесач

director

režiser

режисер

documentary

dokumentarac

документарац

drama

drama

драма

drummer

bubnjar

бубњар

duet

duo/ duet

дуо/ дует

episode

epizoda

епизода

event

događaj

догађај

exhibit

eksponat

експонат

exhibition

izložba

изложба

fair

sajam

сајам

fantasy

fantazija

фантазија

feature/ feature film

svojstvo/ igrani film

својство/ играни филм

film

film

филм

flick

film

филм

folk

folk

фолк

gallery

galerija

галерија

genre

žanr

жанр

gig

gaža

гажа

group

grupa

група

guitar

gitara

гитара

guitarist

gitarista

гитариста

hip-hop

hip-hop

хип-хоп

horror

horror

хорор

inspirational

inspirativno

инспиративно

jingle

pjesmica

пјесмица

legend

legenda

легенда

lyrics
tekst
текст

magician
mađioničar
мађионичар

microphone
mikrofon
микрофон

motion picture
film
филм

movie director
režiser filma
режисер филма

movie script
scenarij
сценариј

museum
muzej
музеј

music
muzika
музика

musical

mjuzikl

мјузикл

musician

muzičar

музичар

mystery

misterija

мистерија

new age

novo doba

ново доба

opera

opera

опера

opera house

zgrada opere

зграда опере

orchestra

orkestar

оркестар

painter

slikar

сликар

painting

slika

слика

parade

parada

парада

performance

izvedba/ perfomans

изведба/ перфоманс

pianist

pijanista

пијаниста

picture

fotografija

фотографија

play

predstava

представа

playwright

dramaturg

фраматург

pop

pop

поп

popcorn

kokice

кокице

producer

producent

продуцент

rap

rep

реп

reggae

rege

реге

repertoire

repertoar

репертоар

rock

rok

рок

role

uloga

улога

romance

romantika

романтика

scene

scena

сцена

science fiction

naučna fantastika

начна фантастика

sculptor

vajar

вајар

shot

snimak

снимак

show

predstava/ šou

представа/ шоу

show business

šou biznis

шоу бизнис

silent film

nijemi film

нијеми филм

singer

pjevač

пјевач

sitcom

sitkom/ situacijska komedija

ситком/ ситуацијска комедија

soloist

solista

солиста

song

pjesma

пјесма

songwriter

tekstopisac

текстописац

stadium

stadion

стадион

stage

scena/ stejdž

сцена/ стејдж

stand-up comedy

stand-up komedija

станд-уп комедија

television

televizija

телевизија

TV show

TV šou

ТВ шоу

---

theater

Teatar/ pozorište

Театар/ позориште

---

understudy

dubler/ zamjenik glumca

дублер/ замјеник глумца

---

vocalist

vokalist

вокалист

---

violinist

violinist

виолинист

Related Verbs
Povezani glagoli
Повезани глаголи

to act

glumiti

глумити

---

to applaud

aplaudirati

аплаудирати

---

to conduct

dirigovati

дириговати

to dance

plesati

плесати

to direct

režirati

режирати

to draw

nacrtati

нацртати

to entertain

zabaviti

забавити

to exhibit

izlagati

излагати

to host

ugostiti

угостити

to paint

slikati

сликати

to perform

izvesti

извести

to play

igrati

играти

to sculpt

vajati

вајати

to show

pokazati

показати

to sing

pjevati

пјевати

to star

glumiti/ biti zvijezda

глумити/ бити звијезда

to watch

gledati

гледати

Mark Jones is a **legend** in **show business**. His career has been nothing less than amazing. He is an award-winning **actor, director,** and **producer** of **film** and **television**. Jones was born in West Central, California. His mother was a teacher and his father was a police officer. He came from humble beginnings and built his career from the bottom up. As a boy, he loved to be the center of attention; he either had a **microphone** in his hand or a **guitar** over his shoulder. He was a very talented **musician** and it seemed he was headed on a path towards becoming a **singer**. He is a talented **songwriter** as well. Few people know that he released his first and only **album** when he was just 16 years old. It was a **pop album**, but It didn't have much success. That didn't stop him from finding his purpose. He also tried **stand-up comedy**. He always drew large crowds, but he knew that wasn't what he was called to do. When he was in his early twenties, he decided to try out for the local community **musical**. He was amazing in his **role** and that is when he made the decision to try acting and he has never looked back! His acting career took off fast. He got his start on a **sitcom** called *Best Friends.* That show was very popular and aired for eight full seasons. It was the beginning of Jones' long and successful and career. He went on to star in several **feature films,** such as *The Dollar*, *Money Maze*, and *Backyard Boys*, just to name a few. There were a few flops in his career, but that didn't stop him. He has starred in many different **genres** of films; proving his versatility as an **actor**. He has played in **dramas**, **comedies**, and **documentaries**. He has also won multiple major awards for his acting. As time went on, he decided to try **directing films**. He was amazing as a **director** and won awards for his work with **feature films**, such as *The Child* and *End of All.* But that wasn't enough for Mark; he became a **producer** and to no surprise, was very successful. His **films** have been wildly successful and it makes everyone wonder where he will go next. It is safe to call Mark Jones a mega-**star**. He has not only been successful in every **entertainment** venture he has attempted, he has also been successful with his family. He has been married to his wife for twenty-five years, which is a rarity in show business.

Mark Džones je **legenda šou biznisa**. Njegova karijera nije ništa manje nego nevjerovatna. On je nagrađivani **glumac**, red**itelj** i filmski i televizijski **prodcent**. Džones je rođen u Vest Centralu, u Kaliforniji. Njegova majka je bila učiteljica, a njegov otac policajac. On je krenuoodskromnog početka i izgradio svoju karijeru od dna premavrhu. Kao dječak, volio je biti u centru pažnje; ili je imao **mikrofon** u ruci ili **gitaru** preko ramena. Bio je vrlo talentovan **muzičar** i činilo se da je na putu da postane **pjevač**. On je takođe i talentovan **tekstopisac**. Malo ljudi zna da je svoj prvi i jedini **album** objavio kada je imao samo 16 godina. To je bio **pop album**, ali nije imao mnogo uspijeha. To ga nije spriječilo da pronađe svoj cilj. Također se okušao i u **stand-up komediji**. On je uvijek privlačio veliki broj ljudi, ali je znao da to nije ono što on hoćeda radi. U ranim dvadesetim godinama, odlučio je da se iskuša u **mjuziklu** lokalne zajednice. Bio je nevjerovatan u svojoj **ulozi**, te je tada odlučio da se okuša u glumi i nikada se nije osvrtao nazad! Njegova glumačka karijera jebrzo napredovala. Dobio je svoju prvu uloguu **sitkomu** "Najbolji prijatelji". Ta serija je bila jako popularna i emitovana je punih 8 sezona. To je bio početak Džonesve duge i uspješne karijere. Glumio je u nekoliko **filmova**, kao što su"The Dollar", "Money maze" i "Backyard Boys", na primjer. Bilo je nekoliko padova u njegovoj karijeri, ali ga to nijezaustavilo. Glumio je u mnogim filmovima različitih **žanrova**, dokazao je svoju svestranost kao **glumac**. Igrao je u **dramama, komedijama** i **dokumentarcima**. Osvojio je više velikih nagrada za svoju glumu. Kako je vrijeme prolazilo, odlučio je da pokuša **režirati filmove**. Bio je nevjerovatan kao režiser i osvojio je nagrade za svoj rad nafilmovima, kao što su"Dijete" i "kraj svega". Ali to nije bilo dovoljno za Marka. Postao je **producent** i, bez iznenađenja, veoma uspješan. Njegovi **filmovi** su dostigli nevjerovatan uspjeh i svi su se pitali gdje će ići dalje. Zasigurno možemo Mark Džonesa nazvati mega-**zvijezdom**. On nije samo uspješan u svakom **zabavljačkom** poduhvatu u kojem se okušao, već je uspiješan i u porodičnom životu. U braku je sa svojom suprugomveć dvadeset i pet godina, što je rijetkost u šou biznisu.

Марк Џонес је **легенда шоу бизниса**. Његова каријера није ништа мање него невјероватна. Он је награђивани **глумац, редитељ** и филмски и телевизијски **продуцент**. Џонес је рођен у Вест Централу, у Калифорнији. Његова мајка је била учитељица, а његов отац полицајац. Он је кренуо одскромног почетка и изградио своју каријеру од дна премаврху. Као дјечак, волио је бити у центру пажње; или је имао **микрофон** у руци или **гитару** преко рамена. Био је врло талентован **музичар** и чинило се да је на путу да постане **пјевач**. Он је такође био италентовани **текстописац**. Мало људи зна да је свој први и једини **албум** објавио када је имао само 16 година. То је био **поп албум**, али није имао много успијеха. То га није спријечило да пронађе својциљ. Такођер се окушао и у **станд-уп комедији**. Он је увијек привлачио велики број људи, али је знао да то није оно што онхоћеда ради. У раним двадесетим годинама, одлучио је да се искуша у **мјузиклу** локалне заједнице. Био је невјероватан у својој **улози**, те је тада одлучио да се окуша у глуми и никада се није освртао назад! Његова глумачка каријера је брзо напредовала. Добио је своју прву улогу у **ситкому**"Најбољи пријатељи". Та серијаје била јако популарнаи емитована је пуних 8 сезона. То је био почетак Џонесове дуге и успијешне каријере. Глумиоје у неколико **филмова**, као што су"Тхе Доллар", "Монеу мазе" и "Бацкуард Боус", на примјер. Било је неколико падова у његовој каријери, али га то нијезауставило. Глумио је у многим филмовима различитих **жанрова**, доказао је своју свестраност као **глумац**. Играо је у **драмама, комедијама** и **документарцима**. Освојио је више великих награда за своју глуму. Како је вријеме пролазило, одлучио је да покуша **режирати филмове**. Био је невјероватан као режисер и освојио је награде за свој рад на филмовима, као што су "Дијете" и „Крај свега". Али то није било довољно за Марка. Постао је **продуцент** и, без изненађења, веома успјешан. Његови **филмови** су достигли невјероватан успјех и сви су се питали гдје ће ићи даље. Засигурно можемо Марк Џонеса назвати мега-**звијездом**. Он није само успијешан у сваком **забављачком** подухвату у којем се окушао, већ је успијешан и у породичном животу. У браку је са својом супругомвећ двадесет и пет година, што је ријеткост у шоу бизнису.

10) Games and sport
10) Igre I sportovi
10) Игре и спортови

ace

as

ас

---

amateur

amater

аматер

---

archery

streljaštvo

стрељаштво

---

arena

arena

арена

---

arrow

strijela

стријела

---

athlete

atleta/ atletičar

атлета/ атлетичар

---

badminton

badminton

бадминтон

ball

lopta

лопта

base

baza

база

baseball

bejzbol

бејзбол

basket

koš

кош

basketball

košarka

кошарка

bat

palica

палица

bicycle

biciklo

бицикло

billiards
bilijar
билијар

bow
luk
лук

bowling
kuglanje
куглање

boxing
boks
бокс

captain
kapiten
капитен

champion
šampion/ prvak
шампион/ првак

championship
prvenstvo
првенство

cleats
klinovi
клинови

club
klub
клуб

competition
takmičenje
такмичење

course
kurs
курс

court
igralište
игралиште

cricket
kriket
крикет

cup
kup
куп

curling
karling
карлинг

cycling
biciklizam
бициклизам

darts
pikado
пикадо

defense
odbrana
одбрана

diving
ronjenje/ skokovi s daske
роњење/ скокови с даске

dodgeball
graničar
граничар

driver
vozač
возач

equestrian
jahač
јахач

event
događaj
догађај

fan
fan/ obožavatelj
фан/ обожаватељ

fencing

mačevanje

мачевање

field

polje

поље

figure skating

umjetničko klizanje

умјетничко клизање

fishing

pecanje

пецање

football

fudbal/ nogomet

фудбал/ ногомет

game

Igra/ utakmica

Игра/ утакмица

gear

oprema

опрема

goal

gol

гол

golf
golf
голф

golf club
Palica za golf
Палица за голф

gym
dvorana/ sala za vježbanje
дворана/ сала за вјежбање

gymnastics
gimnastika
гимнастика

halftime
poluvrijeme
полувријеме

helmet
kaciga
кацига

hockey
hokej
хокеј

horse racing
trke konja
трке коња

hunting

lov

лов

ice skating

klizanje na ledu

клизање на леду

inning

utakmice

утакмице

jockey

džokej

джокеј

judo

džudo

джудо

karate

karate

карате

kayaking

kajakaštvo

кајакаштво

kickball

kikbol

кикбол

lacrosse
lakros
лакрос

league
liga
лига

martial arts
borilačke vještine
борилачке вјештине

mat
strunjača
струњача

match
meč
меч

medal
medalja
медаља

net
mreža
мрежа

offense
napad
напад

Olympic Games

Olimpijske igre

Олимпијске игре

pentathlon

petoboj

петобој

pitch

bacanje

бацање

play

igra

игра

player

igrač

играч

polo

polo

поло

pool

bazen

базен

pool cue

štap za bilijar

штап за билијар

professional
profesionalac
професионалац

puck
pak za hokej
пак за хокеј

quarter
četvrtina
четвртина

race
utrka
утрка

race car
auto za utrke
ауто за утрке

racket
reket
рекет

record
rekord
рекорд

referee
sudija
судија

relay

smjena

смјена

riding

jahanje

јахање

ring

ring

ринг

rink

vještačko klizalište

вјештачко клизање

rowing

veslanje

веслање

rugby

ragbi

рагби

running

trčanje

трчање

saddle

sedlo

седло

sailing

jedrenje

једрење

score

skor/ rezultat

скор/ резултат

shuffleboard

šaflbord

шафлборд

shuttle cock

loptica za badminton

лптица за бадминтон

skates

klizaljke

клизаљке

skating

klizanje

клизање

skiing

skijanje

скијање

skis

skije

скије

soccer

nogomet

ногомет

softball

softbol

софтбол

spectators

gledaoci

гледаоци

sport

sport

спорт

sportsmanship

fer igra

фер игра

squash

skvoš

сквош

stadium

stadion

стадион

surf

surfanje

сурфање

surfboard
daska za surfanje
даска за сурфање

swimming
plivanje
пливање

table tennis/ ping pong
stoni tenis/ ping pong
стони тенис/ пинг понг

tag
oznaka
ознака

team
ekipa/ tim
екипа/ тим

tennis
tenis
тенис

tetherball
teterbol
тетербол

throw
bacanje
бацање

track

traka

трака

track and field

atletska staza

атлеткса стаза

volleyball

odbojka

одбојка

water skiing

skijanje na vodi

скијање на води

weight lifting

dizanje tegova

дизање тегова

whistle

zviždaljka

звиждаљка

win

pobjeda

побједа

windsurfing winner

pobjednik jedrenja na vjetru

побједник једрења на вјетру

wrestling
hrvanje
хрвање

Related Verbs
Povezani glagoli
Повезани глаголи

to catch
uhvatiti
ухватити

---

to cheat
varati
варати

---

to compete
takmičiti
такмичити

---

to dribble
driblati
дриблати

---

to go
ići
ићи

---

to hit
pogoditi
погодити

---

to jump

skočiti

скочити

to kick

udariti

ударити

to knock out

nokautirati

нокаутирати

to lose

izgubiti

изгубити

to play

igrati

играти

to race

utrkivati

утркивати

to run

trčati

трчати

to score

postići

постићи

to win

pobjediti

побједити

Sports are an important part of our culture and have been throughout all history. Men specifically, are drawn to **sports** because of their competitive nature. From the time they are four or five years old, little boys are playing **sports** such as **baseball**, **soccer**, and **basketball**. They grow up to be men and their competitive nature grows with them. Contact **sports**, such as American **football, dodgeball, boxing, hockey**, and **wrestling** are popular among men because of their competitiveness. Women also enjoy **sports**, but usually prefer **sports** with less contact, such as **tennis, figure skating, gymnastics**, and **swimming**. In recent years, women are participating in more contact **sports** than ever before. Even retirees enjoy playing **sports**, **games** such as **golf** and **shuffleboard** are popular among the older crowd. Not only do people enjoy playing **sports**, they love to watch **sports** as well. Wherever you travel, you are sure to see a **fan** or two dressed in their favorite **team** colors. **Sports fan** merchandise is a huge industry. **Sports fans** spend a lot of money every year to buy **tickets** to events to cheer on their **team**. The most popular sporting **event** in the world is the **Olympic Games**. Most **athletes** dream of becoming an **Olympic medalist**. Although, there are some similarities, the **event** has changed quite a bit over the years. The **Olympics** have a rich history and began in Greece. **Sports** played an important role in Greek culture; playing a part in religious festivals as well as used as training for the Greek military. The **Olympics** began as a festival of **sporting events** that was very popular among the people; there were over 30 thousand **spectators** in attendance. The

Greeks competed in **track and field events**, such as **running, javelin, long jump, discus,** just to name a few. They also **wrestled** and had **boxing matches**. The most popular event was the **pentathlon**, which included five **events**: the **long jump, javelin, discus,** a foot **race**, and **boxing**. The **Olympic Games** and the **sports** involved have changed since that first **event**. Today's **Olympic Games** are held in a different city each year. Over 10 thousand **athletes** compete in over 300 **events**! Some of the sports in the Modern **Olympic Games** are **archery, diving, basketball, cycling, volleyball, boxing,** and the modern **pentathlon** which includes **fencing, swimming,** show jumping**(equestrian**), pistol **shooting,** and a cross country **run.**

Sport je važan dio naše kulture i uvijek je bio kroz čitavu historiju. Muškarci posebno, su privučeni **sportom** zbog svoje natjecateljske prirode. Od dobi kada imaju četiri ili pet godina, dječaci se baveju **sportovima** poput **bejzbola, nogometa i košarke**. Oni odrastaju u muškarce i njihova natjecateljska priroda raste sa njima. Kontaktni **sportovi**, poput američkog**futbala, graničara, boksa, hokeja i hrvanja** su poplarni među muškarcima zbog njihoveborbenosti. Žene također uživaju u **sportu**, ali uglavnom preferiraju sportovesa manje kontakta, poput **tenisa, umjetničkog klizanja, gimnastike i plivanja**. Posljednjih nekoliko godina žene su učestvovale u više kontaktnih **sportova** nego ikada prije. Čak i penzioneri uživaju baveći se**sportom**, igre poput **golfa i šaflborda** su popularne među starijima. Ne samo da ljudi uživaju baveći se**sportom**, već uživaju i u gledanju **sporta**. Gdje god putujete, sigurno ćete vidjeti **navijača** ili dvojicu obučene u boje njihovog omiljenog **tima**. **Sportska navijačka** opremaje ogromna industrija. **Navijači** troše mnogo novca svake godine kako bi kupili **karte** za utakmicedabi navijali za svoj **tim**. Najpopularniji sportski **događaj** u svijetu su **Olimpijske Igre**. San većine **sportista** je da postanu **Olimpijski medaljisti**. Iako postoje neke sličnosti, ovaj **događaj** se dosta promijenio tokom godina. **Olimpijada** ima bogatu historiju i započela je u Grčkoj. **Sportovi** su imali važnu ulogu u grčkoj kulturi; igrali su ulogu u vjerskim festivalima i koristili kao trening grčke vojske. **Olimpijada** je započela kao festival **sportskih dešavanja** koja su bila veoma popularna među ljudima; bilo je više od 30 000 **gledatelja** u publici. Grci su se natjecali u **atletskim i poljskim događajima** kao što su **trčanje, bacanje koplja, skok u dalj, bacanje diska** i tako dalje. Također su se **hrvali** i imali **boks mečeve**. Najpopularniji događaj je bio **petoboj**, koji je uključivao pet događaja: **skok u dalj, bacanje koplja i diska, trčanje i boks**. **Olimpijske igre i sportovi** koji su uključeni u to su se promijenili od tog prvog **događanja**. Današnje **Olimpijske igre** se održavaju u različitim gradovima svake godine. Preko 10 000 sportista se takmiči u preko 300 **događaja**! Neki od sportova Modernih **Olimpijskih igara** su **streljarstvo, ronjenje, košarka, biciklizam, odbojka, boks**, imoderni **petoboj** koji uključuje mačevanje, **plivanje, preponsko skakanje (konjički), pucanje iz pištolja i kros trčanje**.

Спорт је важан дио наше културе и увијек је био кроз читаву хисторију. Мушкарци посебно, су привучени **спортом** због своје натјецатељске природе. Од доби када имају четири или пет година, дјечаци се баве**спортовима** попут, **ногомета и кошарке**. Они одрастају у мушкарце и њихова натјецатељска природа расте са њима. Контактни **спортови**, попут америчког **фудбала, граничара, бокса, хокеја и хрвања** су попларни међу мушкарцима због њиховеборбености. Жене такођер уживају у **спорту**, али углавном преферирају **спортове**са мање контакта, попут **тениса, умјетничког клизања, гимнастике и пливања**. Посљедњих неколико година жене су учествовале у више контактних **спортова** него икада прије. Чак и пензионери уживају бавећи се**спортом**, игре попут **голфа и шафлборда** су популарне међу старијима. Не само да људи уживају бавећи се**спортом**, већ уживају и у гледању спорта. Гдје год путујете, сигурно ћете видјети **навијача** или двојицу обучене у боје њиховог омиљеног **тима**. **Спортска навијачка роба** је огромна индустрија. **Навијачи** троше много новца сваке године како би купили **карте** за утакмицедаби навијали за свој **тим**. Најпопуларнији спортски **догађај** у свијету су **Олимпијске Игре**. Сан већине **спортиста** је да постану **Олимпијски медаљисти**. Иако постоје неке сличности, овај **догађај** се доста промиенио током година. **Олимпијада** има богату хисторију и започела је у Грчкој. **Спортови** су имали важну улогу у грчкој култури; играли су улогу у вјерским фестивалима и користили као тренинг грчке војске. **Олимпијада** је започела као фестивал **спортских дешавања** која су била веома популарна међу људима; било је више од 30 000 **гледатеља** у публии. Грци су се натјецали у **атлетским и пољцким догађајима** као што су **трчање, бацање копља, скок у даљ, бацање диска**, и тако даље. Такођер су се **хрвали** и имали **бокс мечеве**. Најпопуларнији **догађај** је био **петобој**, који је укључивао пет догађаја: **скок у даљ, бацање копља и диска, трчање и бокс. Олимпијске игре и спортови** који су укључени у то су се промијенили од тог првог догађања. Данашње **Олимпијске игре** се одржавају у различитим градовима сваке године. Преко 10 000 спортиста се такмичи у преко

300 **догађаја!** Неки од спортова Модерних **Олимпијских игара** су **стрељарство, роњење, кошарка, бициклизам, одбојка, бокс и** модерни који укључује**мачевање, пливање, препонско скакање (коњички), пуцање из пиштоља и крос трчање**.

11) Food
11) Hrana
11) Храна

apple

jabuka — ya-boo-ka

јабука

---

bacon

slanina - sla-E-nah

сланина

---

bagel

đevrek Je-V-ĕr-ck

ђеврек

---

banana

banana

банана

---

beans

grah

грах

---

beef

govedina -- gov-et-d-nah

говедина

---

bread

hljeb

хљеб

broccoli

brokule

брокуле

brownie

brauni

брауни

cake

torta

торта

candy

slatkiš

слаткиш

carrot

mrkva

мрква

celery

celer

целер

cheese

sir

сир

cheesecake
tortaod sira
тортаод сира

chicken
pile
пиле

chocolate
čokolada
чоколада

cinnamon
cimet
цимет

cookie
kolačić
колачић

crackers
krekeri
крекери

dip
umak
умак

eggplant
patlidžan
патлиджан

fig

smokva

смоква

fish

riba

риба

fruit

voće

воће

garlic

bijeli luk

бијели лук

ginger

đumbir

ђумбир

ham

šunka

шунка

herbs

začinske biljke

Зачинске биљке

honey

med

мед

ice cream
sladoled
сладолед

jelly/ jam
Žele/ džem
Желе/ джем

ketchup
kečap
кечап

lemon
limun
лимун

lettuce
zelena salata
зелена салата

mahi mahi
mahi mahi
махи махи

mango
mango
манго

mayonnaise
majoneza
мајонеза

meat

meso

месо

melon

dinja

диња

milk

mlijeko

млијеко

mustard

senf

сенф

noodles

rezanci

резанци

nuts

orasi

ораси

oats

zob

зоб

olive

maslina

маслина

orange
naranča
наранча

pasta
tjestenina
тјестенина

pastry
tijesto
тијесто

pepper
biber
бибер

pork
svinjetina
свињетина

potato
krompir
кромпир

pumpkin
bundeva
бундева

raisin
grožđica
грожђица

sage

kadulja

кадуља

---

salad

salata

салата

---

salmon

losos

лосос

---

sandwich

sendvič

сендвич

---

sausage

kobasica

кобасица

---

soup

supa

супа

---

squash

bundeva

бундева

---

steak

odrezak

одрезак

---

strawberry

jagoda

jагода

---

sugar

šećer

шећер

---

tea

čaj

чај

---

toast

tost

тост

---

tomato

paradajz

парадајз

---

vinegar

ocat

оцат

---

vegetables

povrće

поврће

---

water

voda

вода

---

wheat

pšenica

пшеница

yogurt

jogurt

јогурт

Restaurants and Cafes
Restorani I kafići
Ресторани и кафићи

a la carte

a la carte

а ла царте

a la mode

moderno

модерно

appetizer

predjelo

предјело

bar

bar/ šank

бар/ шанк

beverage

piće

пиће

bill
račun
рачун

bistro
bistro
бистро

boiled bowl
kuhana posuda
кухана посуда

braised
pirjani
пирјани

breakfast
doručak
доручак

brunch
užina
ужина

cafe/ cafeteria
kafe/ kafeterija
кафе/ кафетерија

cashier
blagajnik
благајник

chair
stolica
столица

charge
naplatiti
наплатити

check
račun
рачун

chef
kuhar
кухар

coffee
kafa
кафа

coffee shop
kafić
кафић

condiments
začini
зачини

cook
kuhanje
кухање

courses

jela

јела

credit card

kreditna kartica

кредитна картица

cup

šoljica

шољица

cutlery

pribor za jelo

прибор за јело

deli/ delicatessen

delikatese

деликатесе

dessert

desert

десерт

dine

ručati

ручати

diner

restoran, bistro

Ресторан, бистро

dinner

večera

вечера

dish

suđe

суђе

dishwasher

mašinaza pranje suđa

машиназа прање суђа

doggie bag

kesa koja se ponese iz restorana

кеса која се понесе из ресторана

drink

piće

пиће

entree

glavno jelo

главно јело

food

hrana

храна

fork

viljuška

виљушка

glass
čaša
чаша

gourmet
sladokusac
сладокусац

hor d'oeuvre
predjelo
предјел

host/ hostess
domaćin/ domaćica
домаћин/ домаћица

knife
nož
нож

lunch
ručak
ручак

maitre d'
šef sale
шеф сале

manager
menadžer
менаджер

menu

meni

мени

mug

krigla

кригла

napkin

salveta

салвета

order

narudžba

наруджба

party

zabava

забава

plate

tanjir

тањир

platter

pladanj

пладањ

reservation

rezervacija

резервација

restaurant

restoran

ресторан

saucer

tanjurić

тањурић

server

server

сервер

side order

prilog

прилог

silverware

srebrno posuđe

сребрно посуђе

special

posebni

посебни

spoon

kašika

кашика

starters

starteri

стартери

supper

večera

вечера

table

stol

стол

tax

porez

порез

tip

napojnica

напојница

to go

ići

ићи

utensils

posuđe

посуђе

waiter/ waitress

konobar/ konobarica

конобар/ конобарица

Related Verbs
Зovezani glagoli
Повезани глаголи

to bake

ispeći

испећи

to be hungry

biti gladan

бити гладан

to cook

kuhati

кухати

to cut

rezati

резати

to drink

piti

пити

to eat

jesti

јести

to eat out

jesti vani

јести вани

to feed

hraniti

хранити

to grow

rasti

расти

to have breakfast

doručkovati

доручковати

to have lunch

ručati

ручати

to have dinner

večerati

вечерати

to make

napraviti

направити

to order

naručiti

наручити

to pay

platiti

платити

to prepare

pripremiti

припремити

---

to request

zahtijevati

захтијевати

---

to reserve

rezervirati

резервирати

---

to serve

služiti

служити

---

to set the table

postaviti stol

поставити стол

---

to taste

okusiti

окусити

John and Mary have been dating for quite some time now. Next week is their two year anniversary and John wants to make it really special. Mary really enjoys a nice **steak dinner** out, so John is going to make **reservations** at her favorite **restaurant**. She will be so surprised because they haven't eaten there in a while and she just loves their **salad** and **bread**. John calls and speaks to the **manager** ahead of time to set up the **reservation.** Finally, the day arrives and John picks Mary up at her home. She still doesn't know where they are going, but is excited for the surprise. "Where are we going? Mary asked. "I told you, it's a surprise!" said John. So Mary begins trying to guess where their surprise destination is. "Is it our favorite **diner**? I love the laid back atmosphere and the **waitress** is so nice." "Is it the **coffee shop** on the corner? You know how much I love **coffee**." They arrive at the **restaurant** and she squeals with delight at the thought of the **cheesecake** that they serve for **dessert** . The **host** greets them at the door and promptly seats them at their favorite **table** near the **bar**. It is a quiet little corner of the **restaurant**. The server greets them, lays a **napkin** and **silverware** on their **table**, and then takes their **drink order**. She offers them an **appetizer** while they wait. When the **server** returns, she begins to tell the couple about the daily **specials**. "We'll have two of your best steak **dinners.**" John said, "Nothing but the best for my girl!" They are really enjoying their **gourmet meal** and the conversation is great, as always. I think we should have **dessert** for this special night. John tells the **server** that they would like a **brownie a la mode t**o share. The server brings the delicious brownie on a **plate** with two **spoons**. John and Mary both look at the **dessert** and decide they do not have room to eat it. "I think we will need that **to-go,** " said Mary. While waiting for the server to pack up their **doggie bag**, John surprised Mary by getting down on his knee to propose! The whole **restaurant** was clapping; even the **dishwasher** and **cooks** came out to congratulate the couple. What a wonderful second anniversary this turned out to be for the happy couple. Now, every year on their anniversary, they **dine** at their favorite **restaurant** to celebrate such a wonderful evening.

Džon i Meri su već neko vrijeme u vezi. Slijedeće sedmice je njihova druga godišnjica i Džon želi da to bude stvarno posebno. Meri uživa u dobroj **večeri s odreskom,** pa će Džon rezervisati u njenom najdražem **restoranu.** Ona će biti jako iznenađena, jer tamo nisu jeli dugo vremena i ona jako voli njihovu **salatu i hljeb.** Džon je nazvao i razgovarao sa **menadžerom** unaprijedkako bi napravio**rezervaciju.** Napokon, dan stiže i Džon dolazi po Meri ispred njene kuće. Još uvijek ne zna gdje idu, ali je uzbuđena zbog iznenađenja. "Gdje idemo?", pita Meri. "Rekao sam ti, to je iznenađenje!", rekao je Džon. Tako je Meri pokušavala da pogodi njihovu destinaciju iznenađenja. "Je li to naš omiljeni**restoran?** Volim opuštenu atmosferu i **konobarica** je tako fina." "Je li to **kafić** na uglu? Znaš koliko volim **kafu".** Stižu u **restoran,** a ona sa oduševljenjem pomisli na **tortuod sira** koju služe za **desert.** **Domaćin** ih dočekuje pred vratima i odmah smješta za njihov omiljeni **stol** u blizini **šanka.** To je mirni kutak **restorana.** **Poslužiteljica** ih pozdravlja, postavlja **salvetu i srebrno posuđe** na njihov **stol,** a zatim uzima **narudžbu** za **piće.** Nudi im aperitivdok čekaju. Kada se **poslužiteljica** vratila, rekla je paru o **specijalitetima dana:** "Uzet ćemovaša dva najbolja odreska za **večeru".** Džon je rekao: "Ništa osim najboljeg za moju djevojku!" Oni su stvarno uživali u svom **gurmanskom obroku** i razgovor je bio odličan, kao i uvijek. "Mislim da bismo trebali imati **desert** za ovu posebnu noć", rekao je Džon **poslužiteljici** da žele **brauni a la mode** da podijele. **Poslužiteljica** je donijela ukusne braunije na **tanjiru** idvije **kašike.** Džon i Meri su pogledali u **desert** i shvatili da nemaju više prostora za hranu. "Mislim da ćemo to morati ponijeti", rekla je Meri. Čekajući poslužiteljicu da spakira njihovu **kesicu za ponijeti,** Džon je iznenadio Meri kleknuvši na koljena i zaprosivši je! Čitav **restoran** je pljeskao, čak su i **perač suđa** i

kuhari izašli čestitati paru. Kakva je to prekrasna druga godišnjica bila za ovaj sretan par. Sada, svake godine na njihovu godišnjicu, oni **ručaju** u svom omiljenom **restoranu** kako bi proslavili tako predivno veče.

Џон и Мери су већ неко вријеме у вези. Слиједеће седмице је њихова друга годишњица и Џон жели да то буде стварно посебно. Мери ужива у доброј **вечери с одреском**, па ће Џон резервисати у њеном најдражем **ресторану**. Она ће бити јако изненађена, јер тамо нису јели дуго времена и она јако воли њихову **салату и хљеб**. Џон је назвао и разговарао са **менаджером** унаприједкако би направио**резервацију**. Напокон, дан стиже и Џон долази по Мери испред њене куће. Још увијек не зна гдје иду, али је узбуђена због изненађења. "Гдје идемо?", пита Мери. "Рекао сам ти, то је изненађење!", рекао јеЏом. Тако је Мери покушавала да погоди њихову дестинацију изненађења. "Је ли наш омиљениресторан? Волим опуштену атмосферу и **конобарица** је тако фина." "Је ли то **кафић** на углу? Знаш колико волим **кафу**". Стижу у **ресторан**, а она са одушевљењем помисли на **тортуод сира** коју служе за десерт. Домаћин их дочекује пред вратима и одмах смијешта за њихов омиљени **стол** у близини **шанка**. То је мирни кутак **ресторана**. **Послужитељица** их поздравља, поставља **салвету** и **сребрно посуђе** на њихов **стол**, а затим узима **наруджбу** за пиће. Нуди им аперитивдок чекају. Када се вратила, рекла је пару о **специјалитетима дана**: "Узет ћемо вашадва најбоља одреска за **вечеру**". Џон је рекао: "Ништа осим најбољег за моју дјевојку!" Они су стварно уживали у свом **гурманском оброку** и разговор је био одличан, као и увијек. "Мислим да бисмо требали имати

десерт за ову посебну ноћ”, рекао је Џон **послужитељици** да желе **брауни а ла моде** да подијеле. **Послужитељица** је донијела укусне брауније на тањиру идвије кашике. Џон и Мери су погледали у **десерт** и схватили да немају више простора за храну. “Мислим да ћемо то морати понијети”, рекла је Мери. Чекајући **послужитељицу** да спакира њихову кесицу за понијети, Џон је изненадио Мери клекнувши на кољена и запросивши је! Читав **ресторан** је пљескао, чак су и **перач суђа** и **кухари** изашли честитати пару. Каква је то прекрасна друга годишњица била за овај сретан пар. Сада, сваке године на њихову годишњицу, они ручају у свом омиљеном ресторану како би прославили тако предивно вече.

12) Shopping
12) Kupovina
12) Куповина

bags
vrećice
врећице

bakery
pekara
пекара

barcode
barkod
баркод

basket
košarica
кошарица

bookstore
knjižara
књижара

boutique
butik
бутик

browse

razgledavanje

разгледавање

buggy/ shopping cart

kolica

колица

butcher

mesar

месар

buy

kupovina

куповина

cash

novac

новац

cashier

blagajnik

благајник

change

razmjena

размјена

changing room

Kabina za presvlačenje

Кабина за пресвлачење

cheap

jeftino

јефтино

check

provjeriti

провјерити

clearance

rasprodaja

распродаја

coin

novčić

новчић

convenience store

mali dućan

мали дућан

counter

tezga, pult

тезга, пулт

credit card

kreditna kartica

кредитна картица

customers

mušterije

муштерија

debit card
debitna kartica
дебитна картица

delivery
dostava
достава

department store
robna kuća
робна кућа

discount
popust
попуст

discount store
diskont
дисконт

drugstore/ pharmacy
apoteka/ drogerija
апотека/ дрогерија

electronic store
elektronska prodavnica
електронска продавница

escalator
pokretne stepenice
покретне степенице

expensive
skupo
скупо

flea market
Buvlja pijaca
Бувља пијаца

florist
cvjećar
цвјећар

grocery store
mješovita roba
мјештовита роба

hardware
gvožđarija
гвожђарија

jeweler
zlatar
златар

mall
trgovački centar
трговачки центар

market
tržište
тржиште

meat department

mesni odjel

месни одјел

music store

muzička radnja

музичка радња

offer

ponuda

понуда

pet store

prodavnica ljubimaca

продавница љубимаца

purchase

kupnja

купња

purse

torbica

торбица

rack

vješalica

вјешалица

receipt

Račun, priznanica

признаница

return

povrat

поврат

sale

prodaja

продаја

sales person

prodavač

продавач

scale

skala

скала

size

veličina

величина

shelf/ shelves

polica/ police

полица/ полице

shoe store

prodavnica cipela

продавница ципела

shop

šop

шоп

shopping center

šoping centar

шопинг центар

store

dućan

дућан

supermarket

supermarket

супермаркет

tailor

krojač

кројач

till

kasa

каса

toy store

prodavnica igračaka

продавница играчака

wallet

novčanik

новчаник

Wholesale

veleprodaja

велепродаја

Related Verbs
Povezani glagoli
Повезани глаголи

to buy

kupiti

купити

to charge

naplatiti

наплатити

to choose

odabrati

одабрати

to exchange

razmijeniti

размијенити

to go shopping

ići u kupovinu

ићи у куповину

to owe

dugovati

дуговати

to pay

platiti

платити

to prefer

preferirati

префeрирати

to return

vratiti

вратити

to save

uštediti

уштедити

to sell

prodati

продати

to shop

kupovati

куповати

to spend

potrošiti

потрошити

to try on

isprobati

испробати

to want

željeti

жељети

It was just a few weeks until Christmas and Mark needed to **purchase** a gift for his wife. He didn't know what he was going to get for her. First, he went to the **bookstore**, she loved to read books. He checked the **shelves** to see if he could find something she had not read before, but he had no luck with that. Then he decided to visit her favorite clothing **boutique**. The **salesperson** was very friendly and helpful as he shopped. She knew his wife and was able to help him with **sizes**. He **browsed** the **racks** for just the right gift, but he did not find anything he thought she would like. Besides, everything was so **expensive**! Next, he went to the **shoe store**. He looked around and just couldn't decide what to get for her, so he left that **store**. He resisted going to the **hardware store**, that is his favorite. He thought to himself, "I have to remember, I am **shopping** for my wife, not me!" He finally decided to go to the **mall**. There are plenty of **shops** there! As he walked through the **mall**, he was getting discouraged; he passed a couple of **department stores**, a **music store** and a **toy store**, but nothing seemed right. Finally, he came upon a **jeweler.** His wife loves jewelry. He approached the **counter** and began telling the **salesman** about his wife and the type of jewelry she wears. He was so excited to learn that the ring he picked out was on **sale**. The **salesman** told him the total and Mark reached for his **wallet** to get the **cash**. He asked the salesman, "Does that **price** include **tax**?" "Yes, of course", replied the **salesman**. Mark realized he didn't have enough **cash**, so he paid with his **credit card**. The salesman thanked him and gave him the ring and **receipt**. Mark was so pleased to have found a gift for his wife. He stopped by the **florist** on the way home to surprise her with some flowers. As he was leaving the **florist**, his wife called and asked him to stop by the **grocery store** on his way home. Mark decided he could get what he needed from the **convenience store**, so he stopped there, and then headed home to his wife. She was so surprised that he bought her flowers. She had a little surprise for him as well; she had stopped at the **bakery** on her way home from work. He thanked her for her thoughtful surprise. How lucky he felt to be in such a giving marriage!

Bilo je samo nekoliko sedmica do Božića i Mark je morao **kupiti** poklon za svoju ženu. On nije znaošta da joj uzme. Prvo je otišao u **knjižaru**, ona je voljela čitati knjige. Provjerio je **police** da vidi da li može naći nešto što ona već nije čitala, ali nije imao sreće stime. Onda je odlučio da posjeti njen najdraži **butik**. **Prodavačica** je bila prijateljski raspoložena i korisna kada je kupovao. Ona zna njegovu ženu i mogla mu je pomoći sa veličinama. On je **pregledao** police u **potrazi** za pravim darom, ali nije našao ništa što misli da bi se njoj svidjelo. Osim toga, sve je bilo tako **skupo**! Zatim je otišao u **dućan sa cipelama**. Pogledao je oko sebe i jednostavno nije mogao odlučiti šta da uzme za nju, pa je izašao iz dućana. Opirao se da ne ode u **gvožđarsku radnju**, jer je to njegova omiljena. Mislio je u sebi, „Moram upamtiti, **kupujem** za ženu, ne za sebe". Konačno je odlučio otići u **trgovački centar**. Tamo ima mnogo **dućana**! Dok je hodao kroz centar, postajao je obeshrabren. Prošao je nekoliko **marketa**, **muzičke prodavnice** i **prodavnice sa igračkama**, ali ništa se nije činilo dobrim. Konačno, naišaoje nazlataru. On je prišao **pultu** i počeo govoriti **prodavaču** o svojoj ženi i vrsti nakita koji nosi. Bio je toliko uzbuđen što je prsten za koji se on odlučio na **rasprodaji**. **Prodavač**mu je rekao ukupnu cijenu, a Mark je posegnuo za **novčanikom** kako bi uzeo **gotovinu**. Pitao je prodavača „Da li cijena uključuje **porez**?". „Da, naravno", odgovorio je prodavač. Mark je shvatio da nema dovoljno **gotovine**, pa je platio svojom **kreditnom karticom**. Prodavač mu se zahvalio i dao mu prsten i **račun**. Mark je bio toliko zadovoljan što je pronašao prsten za svoju ženu. Zaustavio se kod **cvjećara** na putu kući kako bi ju iznenadio nekim cvijećem. Dok je izlazio iz **cvjećare**, njegova žena ga je nazvala i zamolila da svrati do **trgovine** na putu ka kući. Mark je odlučio da bi mogao uzetiono što mu je potrebno iz **malog dućana**, pa je svratio tamo i krenuo kući svojoj ženi. Ona je bila toliko iznenađena cvijećem. I ona je imala malo iznenađenje za njega također, zaustavila se u **pekari** na putu sa posla kući. On joj se zahvalio za pažljivoiznenađenje. Koliko se osjećao sretno što je u takvom velikodušnom braku!

Било је само неколико седмица до Божића и Марк је морао **купити** поклон за своју жену. Он није знао шта да јој узме. Прво је отишао у **књижару**, она је вољела читати књиге. Провјерио је **полице** да види да ли може наћи нешто што она већ није читала, али није имао среће с тиме. Онда је одлучио да посјети њен најдражи **бутик**. **Продавачица** је била пријатељски расположена и корисна када је куповао. Она зна његову жену и могла му је помоћи са величинама. Он је **прегледао полице** у потрези за правим даром, али није нашао ништа што мисли да би се њој свидјело. Осим тога, све је било тако **скупо**! Затим је отишао у **дућан са ципелама**. Погледао је око себе и једноставно није могао одлучити шта да узме за њу, па је изашао из дућана. Опирао се да не оде **угвожђарску радњу**, јер је то његова омиљена. Мислио је у себи, „Морам упамтити, **купујем** за жену, не за себе“. Коначно је одлучио отићи у **трговачки центар**. Тамо има много **дућана**! Док је ходао кроз центар, постајао је обесхрабрен. Прошао је неколико**маркета**, **музичке продавнице** и **продавнице са играчкама**, али ништа се није чинило добрим. Коначно, наишао је на**златару**. Он је пришао пулту и почео говорити **продавачу** о својој жени и врсти накита који носи. Био је толико узбуђен што је прстен за који се он одлучио на **распродаји**. Продавачму је рекао укупну цијену, а Марк је посегнуо за **новчаником** како би узео **готовину**. Питао је продавача „Да ли цијена укључује **порез**?“. „Да, наравно“, одговорио је **продавач**. Марк је схватио да нема довољно**готовине**, па је платио својом **кредитном картицом**. Продавач му се захвалио и дао му прстен и **рачун**. Марк је био толико задовољан што је пронашао прстен за своју жену. Зауставио се код **цвјећара** на путу кући како би ју изненадио неким цвијећем. Док је излазио из **цвјећаре**, његова жена га је назвала и замолила да сврати до **трговине** на путу ка кући. Марк је одлучио да би могао узети оно што му је потребно из **малог дућана**, па је свратио тамо и кренуо кући својој жени. Она је била толико изненађена цвијећем. И она је имала мало изненађење за њега такођер, зауставила се у **пекари** на путу са посла кући. Он јој се захвалио за пажљиво изненађење. Колико се осјећаосретаним што је у таквом великодушном**браку**!

13) At the Bank
13) U banci
13) У банци

account

Račun

Рачун

APR/ Annual Percentage Rate

GPS/ Godišnji postotak stope

ГСП/ Годишњи постотак стопе

ATM/ Automatic Teller Machine

Bankomat

Банкомат

---

balance

balans

Баланс

---

bank

Banka

Банка

---

bank charges

Bankovna naplata

Банковна наплата

bank draft

Bankovni nacrt

Банковни нацрт

bank rate

Bankovna stopa

Банковна стопа

bank statement

Bankovni izvod

Банковни извод

borrower

Dužnik

Дужник

bounced check

Odbijeni ček

Одбијени чек

cardholder

Vlasnik kartice

Власник картице

cash

Gotovina

Готовина

cashback

Vraćanje novca

Враћање новца

check
ček
чек

---

checkbook
Čekovna knjižica
Чековна књижица

---

checking account
čekovniračun
чековнирачун

---

collateral
Zalog
Залог

---

commission
Provizija
Провизија

---

credit
Kredit
Кредит

---

credit card
Kreditna kartica
Кредитна картица

---

credit limit
Kreditni limit
Кредитни лимит

---

credit rating

Kreditno rangiranje

Кредитно рангирање

currency

Valuta

Валута

debt

Dug

Дуг

debit

Zaduženje

Задужење

debit card

Debitna kartica

Дебитна картица

deposit

Depozit

Депозит

direct debit

Direktno zaduženje

Директно задужење

direct deposit

Direktni depozit

Директни депозит

expense

Trošak

Трошак

fees

Naknada

Накнада

foreign exchange rate

tečaj

течај

insurance

Osiguranje

Осигурање

interest

Kamata

Камата

Internet banking

Internet bankarstvo

Интернет банкарство

loan

Zajam

Зајам

money

Novac

Новац

money market
Novčano tržište
Новчано тржиште

mortgage
Hipoteka
Хипотека

NSF/ Insufficient Funds
Nedovoljna sredstva
Недовољна средства

online banking
Online bankarstvo
Онлине банкарство

overdraft
prekoračenje
прекорачење

payee
Primatelj
Приматељ

pin number
PIN broj
ПИН број

register
Registar
Регистар

savings account
Štedni račun
Штедни рачун

statement
izvod
извод

tax
Porez
Порез

telebanking
Telebank
Телебанк

teller
, šalter, šalterski blagajnik
шалтер, шалтерски благајник

transaction
Transakcija
Трансакција

traveler's check
Putnički ček
Путнички чек

vault
trezor
трезор

withdraw
Povući
Повући

Related Verbs
Povezani glagoli
Повезани глаголи

to borrow
Posuditi
Посудити

to cash
Unovčiti
Уновчити

to charge
Naplatiti
Наплатити

to deposit
Uplatiti
Уплатити

to endorse
Podržati
Подржати

to enter
Unijeti
Унијети

to hold
Čuvati
Чувати

to insure
osigurati
Осигурати

to lend
pozajmiti
позајмити

to open an account
Otvoriti račun
Отворити рачун

to pay
Platiti
Платити

to save
Uštediti
Уштедити

to spend
Potrošiti
Потрошити

to transfer money
Prebaciti novac
Пребацити новац

to withdraw

povući

повући

If you have a job, you will probably want to open a **bank account**. The two most popular **accounts** available are **checking account** and **savings account**. Banks also have many other **account** options, including **credit** lines, **money market accounts, mortgages**, etc. A **checking account** is good for your day-to-day purchases and paying your bills. You usually receive a **check card,** which works similar to a **credit card** for purchases, and a **checkbook** when you open a **checking account**. Your **check card** works like a **credit card**, however it **withdraws** money directly from your **account**. **Checks** are good for paying friends and family, bills, or anytime you have to mail a payment to someone. Most merchant's accept **checks** or **check cards** for payment, so you should not have a problem with everyday purchases with your **checking account**. You can also use your **debit card** to **withdraw cash** from **ATMs**; you will need to set up a **pin number** for **ATM transactions**. Make sure you keep track of your purchases and **withdrawals** using the **check register** because you don't want to be hit with **NSF fees**. As long as you **deposit** more **money** that you take out, you will be safe from **bank fees**. Many **banks** offer **Online Bill Pay**, making it very convenient for you to pay your bills from the comfort of your home, without ever needing to purchase a stamp. Another popular **bank account** is called a **savings account**. A **savings account** is great for long term planning. **Savings accounts** pay you **interest** on the **money** in your **account**. Different **banks** offer different **interest** rates based upon your savings habits and *balance*. This is the

account you want to put money into and only take it out in case of emergency. **Checking** and **savings accounts** work well together and are the most common types of **bank accounts** available. Many savings accounts offer **overdraft** protection for your **checking account**. If you mess up and **withdraw** too much **money**, your **savings account** funds will step in and keep you from being charged **overdraft fees**. **Banks** are a safe way to save and manage your money. There are many safeguards in place to protect your **accounts**. With so many features, such as **online bill pay, telephone banking,** and **direct deposit,** the smart and efficient way to manage your money is with a **bank account.**

Ako imate posao, vjerovatno ćete htjeti otvoriti **bankovni račun.** Dva najpopularnija **računa** dostupna su **tekući račun** i **štedni račun. Banke** također imaju mnoge druge opcije za **račune,** poput **kreditnih linija, računa novčanog tržišta, hipoteka** itd. **Чековнирачун** je dobar za dnevnu kupovinu i plaćanje računa. Obično dobijate **чековнykarticu** koja radi slično kao i **kraditna kartica** za kupovinu i **чековну knjižicu** kada otvorite svoj **чековнирачун. Vašačekovnakartica** radi poput **kreditne kartice,** ali ipak povlači novac direktno preko vašegaračuna. Čekovi su dobri za plaćanje prijateljima i porodici, račune, ili bilo kada kada morate poslati uplatu nekome. Većina prodavača prihvata **čekove** i **čekovnekartice** za plaćanje, tako da ne bi trebali imati problema sa svakodnevnom kupovinom prekočekovnogračuna. Svoju **debitnu karticu** možete koristiti za **podizanje gotovine** na **bankomatima**; morate postaviti svoj **PIN broj** za **bankomatsku transakciju.** Pobrinite seda pratite sve uplate i **povlačenje novca** preko svog **čekovnogregistra**, jer ne želite biti kažnjeni sa **naknadom za nedovoljna sredstva**. Dokle god **uplaćujete** više novca nego što trošite, biti ćete sigurni od **bankovnih naknada**. Mnoge **banke** nude **usluge internet plaćanje računa**, što je vrlo povoljno za vas da platite svoje račune iz udobnosti svog doma, bez potrebe da kupujete poštanske markice. Drugi popularni **bankovni račun** je **štedni račun**. **Štedni račun** je odličanza dugoročno planiranje. **Štedni račun** vam plaća kamate za novac na računu. Različite **banke** nude različite **kamatne stope** na temelju vaših štednih navika i balansa. Ovo je račun na koji želite staviti novac i podići ga u slučaju nužde. **Čekovnii štedni računi** dobro funkcionišu zajedno i to su najčešće vrste **bankovnih računa** koje su dostupne. Mnogi štedni računi nude zaštitu od **prekoračenja** vašeg čekovnogračuna. Ako pogriješite i **povučete** previše **novca**, sredstva sa vašega **štednog računa** će uskočiti i spasiti Vasod**naknada za prekoračenje** . Banke su siguran način da uštedite i upravljate svojim novcem. Postoje mnoge mjere zaštite koje čuvaju Vaše račune. Sa tako mnogo mogućnosti, **internet plaćanje računa, telefonsko bankarstvo i direktni depozit, bankovni račun** je pametan i učinkovit način upravljanja novcem.

Ако имате посао, вјероватно ћете хтјети отворити **банковни рачун**. Два најпопуларнија рачуна **доступна** су **чековни рачун** и **штедни рачун**. Банке такођер имају многе друге опције за **рачуне**, попут **кредитних линија, рачунановчаног тржишта, хипотека** итд. **Чековнирачун** је добар за дневну куповину и плаћање рачуна. Обично добијате **чековнукартицу** која ради слично као и **крадитна картица**, за куповину и **чековну књижицу** када отворите свој **чековнирачун**. Твоја текућа картица ради попут кредитне картице, али ипак повлачи новац директно преко твог **рачуна**. Чекови су добри за плаћање пријатељима и породици, рачуне, или било када када морате послати уплату некоме. Већина продавача прихвата **чекове** и **чековне картице** за плаћање, тако да не би требали имати проблема са свакодневном куповином преко **вашег чековнограчуна**. Своју **дебитну картицу** можете користити за **подизање готовине** на **банкоматима**; морате поставити свој **ПИН број** за **банкоматску трансакцију**. Побрините се да пратите све уплате и **повлачење новца** преко свог **чековног регистра**, јер не желите бити кажњени са **накнадом за недовољна средства**. Докле год **уплаћујете** више новца него што трошите, бити ћете сигурни од **банковних накнада**. Многе банке нуде **услуге интернет плаћање рачуна**, што је врло повољно за вас да платите своје рачуне из удобности свог дома, без потребе дакупујете поштанске маркице. Други популарни **банковни рачун** је **штедни рачун**. **Штедни рачун** је одличанза дугорочно планирање. **Штедни рачун** вам плаћа камате за новац на рачуну. Различите **банке** нуде различите **каматне стопе** на темељу ваших штедних навика и баланса. Ово је рачун на који желите ставити новац и подићи га у случају нужде. **Чековнии штедни рачуни** добро функционишу заједно и то су најчешће врсте **банковних рачуна** који су доступни. Многи **штедни рачуни** нуде заштиту од **прекорачења** вашег чековнограчуна. Ако погријешите и повучете превише новца, средства са **вашегштедног рачуна** ће ускочити и спасити васо**накнада за прекорачење** . Банке су сигуран начин да уштедите и управљате својим новцем. Постоје многе мјере заштите које чувају Ваше рачуне. Са тако много могућности, **интернет плаћање рачуна, телефонско банкарство и директни депозит**, банковни рачун је паметан и учинковит начин управљања новцем.

14) Holidays
14) Praznici
14) Празници

balloons
Baloni
балони

calendar
Kalendar
календар

celebrate
Slaviti
славити

celebration
Proslava
прослава

commemorating
Obilježavanje
обиљежавање

decorations
Dekoracije
декорације

family

Porodica

породица

feast

Gozba

гозба

federal

Federalni

федерални

festivities

Svečanost

свечаност

fireworks

Vatromet

ватромет

first

Prvi

први

friends

Prijatelji

пријатељи

games

Igre

игре

gifts

Pokloni

поклони

heros

Heroji

хероји

holiday

Odmor

одмор

honor

Čast

част

national

Nacionalna

национална

parade

Parada

парада

party

Zabava

забава

picnics

Piknik/ izlet

пикник/ излет

remember
Sjećanje
cjeħање

resolution
Rezolucija
резолуција

traditions
Tradicije
традиције

American Holidays in calendar order:
Američki praznici po kalendarskom redu:
Амерички празници по календарском реду:

New Year's Day
Nova godina
Нова година

Martin Luther King Jr. Day
Dan Martina Luthera Kinga Jr.
Дан Мартина Лутхера Кинга Jr.

Groundhog Day
Dan Groundhoga
Дан Гроундхога

Valentine's Day
Valentinovo
Валентиново

St. Patrick's Day
Sveti Patrik
Свети Патрик

Easter
Uskrs
Ускрс

April Fool's Day
Prvi april
Први април

Earth Day
Dan planete zemlje
Дан планете земље

Mother's Day
Majčin dan
Мајчин дан

Memorial Day
Dan sjećanja
Дан сјећања

Father's Day
Dan očeva
Дан очева

Flag Day
Dan zastave
Дан заставе

Independence Day/ July 4th
Dan nezavisnosti/ 4. juli
Дан независности/ 4. јули

Labor Day
Praznik rada
Празник рада

Columbus Day
Kolumbov dan
Колумбов дан

Halloween
Noć vještica
Ноћ вјештица

Veteran's Day
Dan veterana
Дан ветерана

Election Day
Izborni dan
Изборни дан

Thanksgiving Day
Dan zahvalnosti
Дан захвалности

Christmas
Božić
Божић

Hanukkah

Hanuka

Ханука

New Year's Eve

Doček Nove godine

Дођек Нове године

Related Verbs
Povezani glagoli

Повезани глаголи

to celebrate

Slaviti

Славити

---

to cherish

Njegovati

Његовати

---

to commemorate

Obilježavati

Обиљежавати

---

to cook

Kuhati

Кухати

---

to give

Davati

Давати

---

to go to
Ići
Ићи

to honor
Odati počast
Одати почаст

to observe
Promatrati
Проматрати

to party
Zabavljati se
Забављати се

to play
Igrati
Играти

to recognize
Prepoznavati
Препознавати

to remember
Sjećati
Cjeћamu

to visit
posjetiti
Посјетити

Many cultures and backgrounds are represented in America. With such diversity, Americans **celebrate** many **holidays** throughout the year. There are so many **holidays** on the **calendar**, there is always something to **celebrate**. In January, **New Year's Day** is a big **celebration**, but the real celebrating comes the night before; there are **fireworks** and **parties** that are broadcast all over the world. In February, we celebrate **Valentine's Day**. It is a day that most couples express their love and affection for each other with cards and gifts. In March, we celebrate **St. Patrick's Day**. Many people wear green items and celebrate Irish heritage. **Easter** is usually celebrated in April. It is a Christian **holiday**, but has also become a secular **holiday** celebrating the beginning of springtime. One of the most cherished **holidays** in America is **Mother's Day**. We honor and remember our mothers and grandmothers on this day; showering them with cards, gifts, and affection. Another big **holiday** in May is **Memorial Day**; originally declared as a day to remember our fallen **heroes** of the various branches of the United States military. It is now seen as the unofficial start of summertime and is celebrated with **picnics** and time with **family**. In June, we **celebrate Father's Day**, while it is not as popular as **Mother's Day**, the idea is the same; to **honor** and **remember** our fathers and grandfathers. In July we **celebrate Independence Day**, also known as **July 4th**. This is the day we **celebrate** our independence from England so many years ago. We **celebrate** with **fireworks** and **picnics** with **family** and **friends**. September brings **Labor Day**, the official end of summer. It was originally declared as a day to recognize the achievements of American workers in our economic successes. In October, we celebrate **Halloween**. Children dress up in their favorite costumes and go trick-or-treating for candy; many adults participate in the fun and have dress-up **parties**. In November, we celebrate **Thanksgiving Day**. It is a day to remember the early settlers to the new world and their achievements. We gather with **family** and **friends** to **feast** on turkey and other comfort-type foods. In December, we **celebrate Christmas Day**. **Christmas** is a Christian **holiday** that **celebrates** the birth of Jesus Christ. It is also **celebrated** by non-Christians and has many secular-type **celebrations** and **traditions**. Santa Claus visits young children on **Christmas Eve**, leaving toys and games in their stocking. **Hanukkah** is another **holiday celebrated** in December by the Jewish community; an eight-day **holiday commemorating** the rededication of the Holy Temple in Jerusalem. This is only a handful of the **holidays celebrated** by Americans. With so many **holidays**, Americans always have a reason to celebrate; so get out the **decorations**, **balloons**, and **games** and let the **festivities** begin!

Mnoge kulture i porijeklasu predstavljena u Americi. Sa takvom raznolikošću, Amerikanci **slave** mnoge **praznike** tokom čitave godine. Postoji toliko mnogo **praznika** na **kalendaru**, uvijek ima nešto da se **slavi**. U januaru, **Nova godina** je veliko **slavlje**, ali stvarno slavlje dolazi noć prije - **vatromet i zabave** se prikazujuu čitavom svijetu. U februaru slavimo **Valentinovo**. To je dan kada većina parova izražava svoju ljubav i privrženost jedni prema drugima sa čestitkamai poklonima. U martu slavimo **Dan Svetog Patrika**. Mnogi ljudi nose zelene stvari i slave irsko naslijeđe. **Uskrs** se obično slavi u aprilu. To je kršćanski **praznik**, ali je postao i sekulani **praznik** koji slavipočetaк proljeća. Jedan od najčešće slavljenih **praznika** u Americi je **Dan majki**. Mi odajemo počast i sjećamo se naših majki i baka na ovaj dan; zasipajući ih porukama, poklonima i privrženošću. Slijedeći veliki **praznik** u maju je **Dan Sjećanja** koji je originalno proglašenkao dan sjećanja na naše pale **heroje** u raznim vidovima oružanih snagaSjedinjenih Američkih Država. Danas ga vide kao neslužbenipočetak ljeta i slavi se izletovanjemi vremenom provedenim sa porodicom. U junu slavimo **Dan Očeva**, iako ovaj dan nije popularan kao **Dan Majki**, ideja je ista: **odati počast** i **sjetiti se** naših očeva i djedova. U julu **slavimo Dan Nezavisnosti**, poznat kao **4. juli**. Ovo je dan kada **slavimo** našu nezavisnost od Engleske koju smo dobili prije mnogo godina. **Slavimo** ga sa **vatrometom** izletima sa porodicom i prijateljima. Septembar nam donosi **Dan Rada**, službenikraj ljeta. Originalno je proglašen kao dan priznavanjapostignuća američkih radnika u našimekonomskim uspjesima. U oktobru slavimo **Noć Vještica**. Djeca se oblače u svoje omiljene kostime i idu odkuće do kuće po slatkiše, mnogi odrasli ljudi učestvuju u zabavi i prave**maskenbale**. U novembru slavimo **Dan Zahvalnosti**. To je dan kada se prisjećamo ranih naseljenikanovog svijeta i njihovih dostignuća. Okupljamo se sa **porodicom i prijateljima** na **gozbi** uz puretinu i drugatradicionalnajela. U decembru **slavimo Božić**. **Božić** je kršćanski **praznik** koji **slavi** rođenje Isusa Krista. Njega **slave** i nekršćani i ima mnogo sekularističkih vrsta **proslava i tradicija**. Djed Mraz posjećuje malu djecu na **božićno veče**, ostavljajući igračke i igrice u njihovim čarapama. **Hanuka** je još jedan **praznik koji se slavi** udecembru od straneJevrejske zajednice, osmodnevni **praznik** kojim se **obilježava** ponovno posvećenje Svetog hrama u Jeruzalemu. Ovo je samo šačica **praznika** koje **slave** Amerikanci. Uz tolikomnogo **praznika**, Amerikanci uvijek imaju razloga da slave, paiznesite**dekoracije, balone i igrice** i neka **svečanosti** počnu!

Многе културе и поријекласу представљена у Америци. Са таквом разноликошћу, Американци **славе** многе **празнике** током читаве године. Постоји толико много **празника** на **календару**, увијек има нешто да се **слави**. У јануару, **Нова година** је велико **славље**, али стварно славље долази ноћ прије - **ватромет и забаве** се приказујуу читавом свијету. У фебруару славимо **Валентиново**. То је дан када већина парова изражава своју љубав и привреженост једни према другима са честиткамаи поклонима. У марту славимо **Дан Светог Патрика**. Многи људи носе зелене ствари и славе ирско наслијеђе. **Ускрс** се обично слави у априлу. То је кршћански **празник**, али је постао и секулани **празник** који славипочетак прољећа. Један од најчешће слављених **празника** у Америци је **Дан мајки**. Ми одајемо почаст и сјећамо се наших мајки и бака на овај дан; засипајући их порукама, поклонима и привреженошћу. Слиједећи велики **празник** у мају је **Дан Сјећања** који је оригинално прглашенкао дан сјећања на наше пале хероје у разним видовима оружаних снагаСједињених Америчких Држава. Данас га виде као неслужбенипочетак љета и слави се излетовањеми временом проведеним са породицом. У јуну славимо **Дан Очева**, иако овај дан није популаран као **Дан Мајки**, идеја је иста: **одати почаст и сјетити се** наших очева и дједова. У јулу **славимо Дан Независности**, познат као **4. јули**. Ово је дан када **славимо** нашу независност од Енглеске коју смо добили прије много година. **Славимо** га са **ватрометом** и излетима са породицом и пријатељима. Септембар нам доноси **Дан Рада**, службеникрај љета. Оригинално је прглашен као дан признавањапостигнућа америчких радника у нашимекономским успјесима. У октобру славимо **Ноћ Вјештица**. Дјеца се облаче у своје омиљене костиме и иду од куће до куће по слаткише, многи одрасли људи учествују у забави и праве маскенбале. У новембру славимо **Дан Захвалности.** То је дан када се присјећамо раних насељеника нового свијета и њихових достигнућа. Окупљамо се са **породицом** и **пријатељима** на **гозби** уз пуретину и друга традиционална јела. У децембру **славимо Божић. Божић** је кршћански **празник** који **слави** рођење Исуса Криста. Њега **славе** и некршћани и има много секуларистичких врста **прослава** и **традиција**. Дјед Мраз посјећује малу дјецу на **божићно вече**, остављајући играчке и игрице у њиховим чарапама. **Ханука** је још један празник који се слави у децембру од стране Јеврејске заједнице, осмодневни празник којим се обиљежава поновно посвећење Светог храма у Јерузалему. Ово је само шачица **празника** које **славе** Американци. Уз толико много **празника**, Американци увијек имају разлога да славе, пада изнесите **декорације, балоне** и **игрице** и нека свечаности почну!

15) Traveling
15) Putovanje
15) Путовање

airport

Aerodrom

Аеродром

backpack

Ruksak

Руксак

baggage

Koferi

Кофери

boarding pass

Prelazak granice

Прелазак границе

business class

Poslovna klasa

Пословна класа

bus station

Autobusna stanica

Аутобусна станица

carry-on
Ručna prtljaga
Ручна пртљага

check-in
Prijava
Пријава

coach
Prevoznik
Превозник

cruise
Krstarenje
Крстарење

depart/ departure
Polazak/ odlazak
Полазак/ долазак

destination
Destinacija
Дестинација

excursion
Ekskurzija
Екскурзија

explore
Istraživanje
Истраживање

first class
Prva klasa
Прва класа

flight
Let
Лет

flight attendant
Stjuart
Стјуарт

fly
Letjeti
Летјети

guide
Vodič
Водич

highway
Autocesta
Аутоцеста

hotel
Hotel
Хотел

inn
Gostionica
Гостионица

journey

Putovanje

Путовање

land

Zemlja

Земља

landing

Slijetanje

Слијетање

lift-off

polijetanje

полијетање

luggage

Prtljaga

Пртљага

map

Karta

Карта

move

Kretanje

Кретање

motel

Motel

Мотел

passenger
Putnik
Путник

passport
Pasoš
Пасош

pilot
Pilot
Пилот

port
Luka
Лука

postcard
Razglednica
Разгледница

rail
Željeznički
Жељезички

railway
Željeznička
Жељезничка

red-eye
Noćni let
Ноћни лет

reservations

Rezervacija

Резервација

resort

Odmaralište

Одмаралиште

return

Povratak

Повратак

road

Cesta

Цеста

roam

Skitanje

Скитање

room

Soba

Соба

route

Ruta

Рута

safari

Safari

Сафари

sail
Jedro
Jедро

seat
sjedište
Cjедиште

sightseeing
rezgledavanje
Разгледавање

souvenir
Suvenir
Сувенир

step
Korak
корак

suitcase
Kofer
Кофер

take off
Poletjeti
Полетјети

tour
Obilazak
Обилазак

tourism
Turizam
Туризам

tourist
Turista
Туриста

traffic
Promet/ saobraćaj
Промет/ saobraćaj

trek
Seoba
Сеоба

travel
Putovanje
Путовање

travel agent
Turistički agent
Туристички агент

trip
Putovanje
Путовање

vacation
Odmor
Одмор

voyage

Putovanje

Путовање

Modes of Transportation
Način prevoza
Начин превоза

airplane/ plane

Avion

Авион

---

automobile

automobil

Аутомобил

---

balloon

Balon

Балон

---

bicycle

biciklo

Бицикло

---

boat

Brod

Брод

---

bus

Autobus

Аутобус

---

canoe

Kanu

Кану

car

Auto

Ауто

ferry

Trajekt

Трајект

motorcycle

Motor

Мотор

motor home

Motorna kuća

Моторна кућа

ship

Brod

Брод

subway

Metro

Метро

taxi

Taksi

Такси

train

Voz

Воз

---

van

Kombi

Комби

Hotels

Hoteli

Хотели

accessible

Dostupan

Доступан

---

airport shuttle

Prevoz do zračne luke

Превоз до зрачне луке

---

all-inclusive

Sveobuhvatan

Свеобухватан

---

amenities

Sadržajan

Садржајан

---

balcony

Balkon

Балкон

---

bathroom

Kupaonica

Купаоница

beach

plaža

Плажа

beds

Kreveti

кревети

bed and breakfast

pansion

пансион

bellboy/ bellhop

Portir/ nosač

Портир/ носач

bill

Račun

Рачун

breakfast

Doručak

Доручак

business center

Poslovni centar

Пословни центар

cable/ satellite tv
Kablovska/ satelitska televizija
Кабловска/ сателитска телевизија

charges (in-room)
Troškovi (u sobi)
Трошкови (у соби)

check-in
Prijava
Пријава

check-out
Odjava
Одјава

concierge
Vratar
Вратар

Continental breakfast
Kontinentalni doručak
Континентални доручак

corridors (interior)
hodnici(interijer)
ходници(интеријер)

doorman
Vratar
Вратар

double bed

Bračni krevet

Брачни кревет

double room

Dvokrevetna soba

Двокреветна соба

elevator

Lift

Лифт

exercise/ fitness room

Fitnes soba

Фитнес соба

extra bed

Pomoćni ležaj

Промоћни лежај

floor

Sprat

Спрат

front desk

Recepcija

Рецепција

full breakfast

Puni doručak

Пуни доручак

gift shop
Dućan za poklone
Дућан за поклоне

guest
Gost
Гост

guest laundry
Praonica za goste
Праоница за госте

hair dryer
Fen za kosu
Фен за косу

high-rise
Visokouzlazni
Високоузлазни

hotel
Hotel
Хотел

housekeeping
Čuvanje kuće
Чување куће

information desk
Infopult
Инфопулт

inn
Gostionica
Гостионица

in-room
U sobi
У соби

internet
Internet
Интернет

iron/ ironing board
Pegla/ daska za peglanje
Пегла/ даска за пеглање

key
Ključ
Кључ

king bed
Francuski krevet
Француски кревет

lobby
Lobi
Лоби

local calls
Lokalni pozivi
Локални позиви

lounge
Čekaonica
Чекаоница

luggage
Prtljaga
Пртљага

luxury
Luksuz
Луксуз

maid
Sobarica
Собарица

manager
upravnik
управник

massage
Masaža
Масажа

meeting room
Sala za sastanke
Сала за састанке

microwave
Mikrovalna
Микровална

mini-bar
Minibar
Минибар

motel
Motel
мотел

newspaper
Novine
Новине

newsstand
Trafika
трафика

non-smoking
Nepušački
Непушачки

pets/ no pets
Ljubimci/ bez ljubimaca
Љубимци/ без љубимаца

pool - indoor/ outdoor
Bazen – otvoreni/ zatvoreni
Базен – отворени/ затворени

porter
nosač
носач

queen bed
Kraljevski krevet
Краљевски кревет

parking
Parking
Паркинг

receipt
Potvrda
Потврда

reception desk
Recepcija
Рецепција

refrigerator (in-room)
frižider(u sobi)
фрижидер

reservation
Rezervacija
Резервација

restaurant
Restoran
Ресторан

room
Soba
Соба

room number

Broj sobe

Број собе

room service

Sobna posluga

Собна послуга

safe (in-room)

Sef (u sobi)

Сеф (у соби)

service charge

Naknada za uslugu

Накнада за услугу

shower

tuš

Туш

single room

Jednokrevetna soba

Једнокреветна соба

suite

Apartman

Апартман

tax

Porez

Порез

tip
Napojnica
Напојница

twin bed
Bračni krevet
Брачни кревет

vacancy/ no vacancy
Upražnjeno/ neupražnjeno
Упражњено/ неупражњено

wake-up call
Poziv za buđenje
Позив за буђење

whirlpool/ hot tub
Vruća kadica
Вруђа кадица

wireless high-speed internet
Bezični internet
Безични интернет

Related Verbs
Povezani glagoli
Повезани глаголи

to arrive
stići
Стиħи

to ask
Pitati
Питати

to buy
Kupiti
Купити

to catch a flight
Uhvatiti let
Ухватити лет

to change
Zamjeniti
Замијенити

to drive
Voziti
Возити

to find
Naći
наћи

to fly
Letjeti
Летјети

to land
Sletjeti
Слетјети

to make a reservation
Rezervisati
Резервисати

to pack
Pakovati
Паковати

to pay
Platiti
Платити

to recommend
Preporučiti
Препоручити

to rent
Iznajmiti
Изнајмити

to see
Vidjeti
Видјети

to stay
odsjesti
одсјести

to take off
Skinuti
Скинути

to travel

Putovati

Путовати

---

to swim

Plivati

Пливати

Michael is young and adventurous and loves to **travel**; ever since he was a little boy, he has enjoyed the excitement of **traveling**. Whether he **travels** by **boat**, **car**, or **plane**; he always has a great time. Michael has **traveled** all over the world on **vacation**. Once, he took a **bus** from Florida to California, just to say he had done so. His wife enjoys **traveling** with Michael; however, she is not an adventurous person. She likes to **vacation** in nice, quiet places. She prefers an easy **trip** that does not require **layovers** or complicated **itineraries**. Her favorite **destination** is Hawaii, so Michael decided to take her there for their anniversary. They made their **reservations** and took a **plane** from California to Hawaii; or so they thought. That is where this **journey** begins. They bought **tickets** on the **red-eye flight** to get an early start on **vacation**. They arrived at the **airport**, got their **luggage checked-in** and with their **carry-on bags** in hand, they headed towards the **concourse**, ready to **fly** away into the sunset! They were in such a hurry to get to their **destination**; they unknowingly **boarded** the wrong **plane**. They both slept during the **flight** and when they arrived, they both felt something was not quite right; they had traveled to **Alaska**! They checked with their **travel agency** and found out there were no **flights** leaving that **airport** until the next morning. Determined to get to their **vacation** in Hawaii,

317

the couple decided to do whatever it took to get there! They took a **ferry** to the nearest **car** rental location and decided to **drive** as much of the way as possible; they would figure the rest out later. They picked up a **map** and headed on their way. They figured they would get to do some **sightseeing** along the way, if nothing else. It was a long **drive**; they drove for hundreds of miles until they just couldn't drive anymore, so they stopped at a **hotel** to get some rest. The next morning, they **checked-out** of their **hotel room** and continued driving. Their **travel agent** called them and said that they had **coach tickets** the next morning, leaving out of LAX **airport**; they just had to be there in time. The couple made it to the **airport** with just ten minutes to spare! They finally **boarded** their **flight**, on their way to Hawaii. When they arrived at the **airport**, they were so relieved to finally be on **vacation**! They took a **shuttle** to the **resort** and finally were able to enjoy a nice, relaxing **vacation**. Of all Michael's **travels**, this was the most adventurous one yet!

Mihajl je mlad i avanturista, i voli da **putuje**; otkad je bio mali dječak, uživao je u uzbuđenju **putovanja**. Bilo da **putuje brodom, autom** ili **avionom**, uvijek se dobro provodio. Mihajl je **putovao** širomsvijeta na **odmore**. Jednom je sjeo na autobus od Floride do Kalifornije, samo da kaže da je to uradio. Njegova suprugauživa putovati sa Mihajlom, ali ona nijeavanturista. Ona voli da **odmara** na lijepim i mirnim mjestima. Preferira lagana **putovanja** koja ne zahtijevaju **odmaranja**i komplicirane **planove putovanja**. Njena omiljena **destinacija** su Havaji, pa je Mihajl odlučio da je povede tamo za njihovu godišnjicu. Oni su napravili **rezervaciju** i sjeli na**avion** izKalifornije do Havaja, ili su bar tako mislili.

Ovdjenjihovo **putovanje** počinje. Kupili su **karte** za **noćni let** kako bi njihov **odmor** što prije počeo. Stigli su na **aerodrom**, obavili**prijavu prtljage** i sa **malim torbama**u rukama, krenuli su prema **prolazu**, spremni **odletjeti** u zalazak sunca! Bili su u takvoj žurbi da dođu do svoje **destinacije** da su se nesvjesno ukrcaliu pogrešan avion. Oboje su spavali tokom **leta**, a kada su stigli, osjetili su da nešto nije u redu. Doputovali su na Aljasku! Provjerili su sa svojom **putničkom agencijom** i saznali da nije bilo **letova** koji polijećusa toga**aerodroma** do slijedećeg jutra. Odlučni da odmor provedu na Havajima, par je odlučio uraditi sve što je trebalo da bi stigli tamo. Oni su se **trajektom** prebacili do najbližeg rent-a-carai odlučili su da **voze** štoje moguće dalje; ostatak će smisliti kasnije. Uzeli su **mapu** i krenuli na put. Shvatili su da će uspjeti da **razgledaju** usput, ako ništa drugo. To je bila duga **vožnja**. Vozili su se stotinama kilometara dok jednostavno nisu više mogli da voze, pa su se zasutavili u **hotelu** kako bi se odmorili. Slijedeće jutro su se **odjavili** iz **hotelske sobe** i nastavili voziti. **Njihov putnički agent** ih je nazvao i rekao da imaju karte za **ekonomsku klasu** za let slijedećo jutro i da trebaju krenutisa LAX **aerodroma**, samo moraju biti tamo na vrijeme. Par je stigao do **aerodroma** samo 10 minuta ranije! Napokon su se **ukrcali** na svoj **let**, na putu ka Havajima. Kad su stigli na **aerodrom**, toliko im je laknulo da su konačno na odmoru! Uzeli su prevoz do odmaralištai konačno bili u mogućnosti da uživaju u lijepom i opuštajućem **odmoru**. Od svih Mihajlovih **putovanja**, ovo je bilonajodvažnije do sad.

Михајл је млад и авантуриста, и воли да **путује**; откад је био мали дјечак, уживао је у узбуђењу **путовања**. Било да **путује бродом, аутом** или **авионом**, увијек се добро проводио. Михајл је **путовао**широмсвијета на **одморе**. Једном је сјео на аутобус од Флориде до Калифорније, само да каже да је то урадио. Његова супругауживаа путовати са Михајлом, али она није авантуриста. Она воли да **одмара** на лијепим и мирним мјестима. Преферира лагана путовања која не захтијевају **одмарања**и комплициране **планове путовања**. Њена омиљена **дестинација** су Хаваји, па је Михајл одлучио да је поведе тамо за њихову годишњицу. Они су направили **резервацију** и сјели на авион из Калифорније до Хаваја, или су бар тако мислили. Овдјењихово **путовање** почиње. Купили су **карте** за **ноћни лет** како би њихов **одмор** што прије почео. Стигли су на **аеродром**, обавили**пријаву пртљаге** и са **малим торбама**у рукама, кренули су према **пролазу**, спремни **одлетјети** у залазак сунца! Били су у таквој журби да дођу до своје **дестинације** да су се несвјесно укрцалиу погрешан авион. Обоје су спавали током **лета**, а када су стигли, осјетили су да нешто није у реду. Допутовали су на Аљаску! Провјерили су са својом **путничком агенцијом** и сазнали да није било **летова** који полијећу са тог аеродрома до слиједећег јутра. Одлучни да одмор проведу на Хавајима, пар је одлучио урадити све што је требало да би стигли тамо. Они су се **трајектом** пребацили до најближег рент-а-цара и одлучили су да возе штоје могуће **даље**; остатак ће смислитикасније. Узели су **мапу** и кренули на пут. Схватили су да ће успјети да **разгледају** успут, ако ништа друго. То је била дуга **вожња**. Возили су се стотинама километара док једноставно нису више могли да возе, па су се засутавили у **хотелу** како би се одморили. Слиједеће јутро су се **одјавили** из **хотелске собе** и наставили возити. **Њихов путнички агент** их је назвао и рекао да имају карте за **економску класу** слиједећо јутро и да требају кренутиса ЛАХ **аеродрома**, само морају бити тамо на вријеме. Пар је стигао до **аеродрома** само 10 минута раније! Напокон су се **укрцали** на свој **лет**, на путу ка Хавајима. Кад су стиглиха аеродром, толико им је лакнуло да су коначно на одмору! Узели су превоз до одмаралиштаи коначно били у могућности да уживају у лијепом и опуштајућем **одмору**. Од свих Михајлових **путовања**, ово је билонајодважније до сада.

16) School
16) Škola
16) Школа

arithmetic

aritmetika

аритметика

---

assignment

zadatak

задатак

---

atlas

atlas

атлас

---

backpack

ruksak

руксак

---

binder

vezač

везач

---

blackboard

tabla

табла

---

book

knjiga

књига

bookbag

torba za knjige

торба за књиге

bookcase

polica za knjige

полица за књиге

bookmark

oznaka

ознака

calculator

digitron

дигитрон

calendar

kalendar

календар

chalk

kreda

креда

chalkboard

ploča

плоча

chart
grafikon
графикон

class clown
razredni kalun
разредни клаун

classmate
drug iz razreda
друг из разреда

classroom
učionica
учиониа

clipboard
oglasnik
огласник

coach
trener
тренер

colored pencils
olovke u boji
оловке у boji

compass
kompas
компас

composition book

sveska s linijama

свеска са линијама

computer

kompjuter

компјутер

construction paper

kolaž papir

колаж папир

crayons

bojice

бојице

desk

stol

стол

dictionary

rječnik

рјечник

diploma

diploma

диплома

dividers

šestar

шестар

dormitory

spavaonica

спаваоница

dry-erase board

suho brisanje table

сухо брисање табле

easel

stalak

сталак

encyclopedia

enciklopedija

енциклопедија

english

engleski jezik

енглески језик

eraser

gumica

гумица

exam

ispit

испит

experiment

eksperiment

експеримент

flash cards

fleš kartice

флеш картице

folder

mapa

мапа

geography

geografija

географија

globe

globus

глобус

glossary

glosar

глосар

glue

ljepilo

љепило

gluestick

ljepilo u tubi

љепило у туби

grades, A, B, C, D, F, passing, failing

ocjene, A-B-C-D-F, prolaženje, padanje

оцјене, А-Б-Ц-Д-Ф, пролажење, падање

gym
gimnastika
гимнастика

headmaster
upravnik
управник

highlighter
marker
маркер

history
historija
хисторија

homework
domaća zadaća
домаћа задаћа

ink
tinta
тинта

janitor
domar
домар

Kindergarten
dječji vrtić
дјечји вртић

keyboard

tastatura

тастатура

laptop

laptop

лаптоп

lesson

lekcija

лекција

library

biblioteka

библиотека

librarian

bibliotekar

библиотекар

lockers

ormarići

ормарићи

lunch

ručak

ручак

lunch box/ bag

lanč paket

ланч пакет

map
karta
карта

markers
markeri
маркери

math
matematika
математика

notebook
sveska
свеска

notepad
bilježnica
биљежница

office
ured
уред

paper
papir
папир

paste
zalijepiti
залијепити

pen
olovka
оловка

pencil
hemijska
хемијска

pencil case
držalo za olovke
држало за оловке

pencil sharpener
šiljalo
шиљало

physical education/ PE
tjelesni odgoj
тјелесни одгој

portfolio
portfolio
портфолио

poster
poster
постер

principal
direktor
директор

professor

profesor

профессор

project

projekt

пројект

protractor

kutomjer

кутомјер

pupil

učenik

ученик

question

pitanje

питање

quiz

kviz

квиз

read

čitati

читати

reading

čitanje

читање

recess

raspust

распуст

ruler

linijar

линијар

science

nauka

наука

scissors

makaze

маказе

secretary

sekretar

секретар

semester

semestar

семестар

stapler

heftalica

хефталица

student

student

студент

tape

traka

трака

teacher

učitelj

учитељ

test

test

тест

thesaurus

leksikon sinonima

лексикон синонима

vocabulary

vokabular

вокабулар

watercolors

vodene bojice

водене бојице

whiteboard

bijeli zaslon

бијели заслон

write

pisati

писати

Related Verbs
Povezani glagoli
Повезани глаголи

to answer

odgovoriti

одговорити

to ask

pitati

питати

to draw

crtati

цртати

to drop out

napustiti

напустити

to erase

obrisati

обрисати

to fail

pasti

пасти

to learn

naučiti

научити

to pass

proći

проћи

to play

igrati

играти

to read

čitati

читати

to register

registrovati

регистровати

to show up

pojaviti se

појавити се

to sign up

prijaviti se

пријавити се

to study

učiti

учити

to teach

podučavati

подучавати

to test

provjeravati

провјеравати

to think

misliti

мислити

to write

pisati

писати

Heather is five years old and has always enjoyed being home with her mom every day. She heard that she would be starting **school** soon and was nervous about it. Summer was coming to an end and Heather was really starting to get anxious about the start of the **school** year. This will be her first and she is unsure about what to expect. She was excited, yet nervous to leave her mom all day. Her mom took her **school supply** shopping on the Saturday before school was to start. She had her list of **school supplies** and was very overwhelmed by all the things in the store. There are so many things on the list, she doesn't know where to start; **crayons**, **paper**, **markers**, **glue**, and more! Heather's mom told her she would need something to put all this stuff in, so she picked out a nice **backpack** with her favorite cartoon cat on it; it also had a matching **lunch bag**! Her mom told her she would also need to get some new clothes because every little girl needs new clothes for the first day of **school**. On the way home from shopping, Heather questioned her mom about **school;** she was getting very excited because she wondered what she would be doing with all this stuff! The first day of **school** finally came and Heather's mom took her to register for the first day of **Kindergarten**. The first stop was the **office**, she met a very nice lady, the **school secretary**, and she also met a handsome gentleman who said he was the **principal** of the **school**. She wasn't sure what that meant, but he must be important. Once everything was settled in the **office**, her mom took her to her new **classroom**. When she walked in, she couldn't believe her eyes; it was amazing! There was a big **chalkboard** on the wall, rows of **desks**, colorful **charts** and **maps**, even some games and **books**. She really likes games and **books**, so she started to relax a bit. Then, she saw her new **teacher**; she was a nice lady, smiling and being very polite. Heather then realized she would be okay. She sent her mom on her way and told her she would see her this afternoon after **school**. She was ready to learn to **read** and **write**, do **math** and **science**; she was not nervous anymore! That day she made several new friends and really like her **teacher**. They had **English** and **Math**; she even got to paint using her new **watercolors**. Heather decided she loved **school** and wanted to come back every day!

Heder imapet godinai uvijek je uživala biti kući sa svojom mamom svaki dan. Ona je čula da će ubrzo krenuti u **školu** i bila je nervozna zbog toga. Ljeto se bližilo kraju i Heder je stvarno postala nestrpljivazbog početka **školske** godine. To će biti njen prvi polazak i ona nije sigurna šta da očekuje. Bila je uzbuđena, ali i nervozna što će ostaviti mamu čitav dan. Mama je odvela u kupovinu **školskog pribora** u subotu prije nego je škola počela. Imala je listu školskih potrepština i bila je preplavljenasvim stvarima u prodavnici. Bilo je toliko stvari na listi, nije znala gdje da počne:**bojice, papir, markeri, ljepilo** i još. Hederina mama rekla je da će trebati nešto u što će staviti sve ove stvari, zato je izabrala lijep ruksak s likom njenenajdraže mačke iz crtića: imala je i odgovarajuću **torbu za užinu**! Mama joj je rekla da treba da nabavi novu odjeću zato što svaka mala djevojčica treba novu odjeću za prvi dan **škole**. Na putu kući iz kupovine, Heder je ispitivala mamu o **školi**: postajala je veoma uzbuđena zato što se pitala šta će da radi sa svim tim stvarima! Prvi dan **škole** je konačno došao i Hederina mama ju je odvela da se prijavi za prvi dan u **dječijem vrtiću**. Prvo zaustavljanje je bio **ured**, upoznala je veoma finu damu, **školsku sekretaricu**, i takođe je upoznala zgodnog džentlmena koji je rekao da je **on školski direktor**.. Nije bila sigurna šta je značilo, ali on je morao biti važan. Kad se sve sredilo u uredu, mama je odvela u njenu novu učionicu. Kada je ušla unutra nije mogla vjerovati svojim očima; bilo je nevjerovatno! Bila je velika **ploča** na zidu, redovi **stolova**, šareni grafikoni i karte, čak i neke igrice i **knjige**. Zaista je voljela igrice i **knjige,** zato je počela da se opušta. Onda je vidjela svoju novu **učiteljicu**, ona je bila finadama, nasmijana i veoma ljubazna. Heder je onda shvatila da će biti u redu. Poslala je mamu kući i rekla da će se vidjeti ovo popodne poslije **škole**. Bila je spremna da uči da **čita** i **piše**, radi **matematiku** i **nauku**; više nije bila nervozna! Taj dan je upoznala još novih prijatelja i zaista joj se svidjela učiteljica. Imali su e**ngleski jezik** i **matematiku**, morala je čak da slika koristeći svoje nove **vodene bojice**. Heder je odlučila da voli **školu** i željela je dolazitisvaki dan!

Хедер имапет година и увијек је уживала бити кући са својом мамом сваки дан. Она је чула да ће убрзо кренути у **школу** и била је нервозна због тога. Љето се ближило крају и Хедер је стварно постала нестрпљивазбог почетка **школске** године. То ће бити њен први полазак и она није сигурна шта да очекује. Била је узбуђена, али и нервозна што ће оставити маму читав дан. Мама је одвела у куповину**школског прибора** у суботу прије него је школа почела. Имала је листу школских потрепштина и била је преплављенасвим стварима у продавници. Било је толико ствари на листи, није знала гдје да почне:**бојице, папир, маркери, љепило** и још. Хедерина мама рекла је да ће требати нешто у што ће ставити све ове ствари, зато је изабрала лијеп руксак с ликом њене најдраже мачке из цртића: имала је и одговарајућу **торбу за ужину**! Мама јој је рекла да треба да набави нови одјећи зато што свака мала дјевојчица треба нову одјећу за први дан **школе**. На путу кући из куповине, Хедер је испитивала маму о **школи**: постајала је веома узбуђена зато што се питала шта ће да ради са свим тим стварима! Први дан **школе** је коначно дошао и Хедерина мама ју је одвела да се пријави за први дан у **дјечијем вртићу**. Прво заустављање је био **уред**, упознала је веома фину даму, **школску секретарицу**, и такођер је упознала згодног џентлмена који је рекао да јеоn **школски директор**. Није била сигурна шта је значило, али он је морао бити важан. Кад се све средило у уреду, мама је одвела у њену нову учионицу. Када је ушла унутра није могла вјеровати својим очима; било је невјероватно! Била је велика **плоча** на зиду, редови **столова**, шарени графикони и карте, чак и неке игрице и **књиге**. Заиста је вољела игрице и **књиге**, зато је почела да се опушта. Онда је видјела своју нову **учитељицу**, она је била финадама, насмијана и веома љубазна. Хедер је онда схватила да ће бити у реду. Послала је маму кућии рекла да ће се видјети ово поподне послије школе. Била је спремна да учи да **чита и пише**, ради **математику** и **науку**; више није била нервозна! Тај дан је упознала још нових пријатеља и заиста јој се свидјела учитељица. Имали су **енглески језик** и **математику**, морала је чак да слика користећи своје нове **водене бојице**. Хедер је одлучила да воли школ и жељела једолазитисваки дан!

17) Hospital
17) Bolnica
17) Болница

ache

bol

бол

---

acute

akutan

акутан

---

allergy/ allergic

alergija/ alergičan

алергија/ алергичан

---

ambulance

hitna pomoć

хитна помоћ

---

amnesia

amnezija

амнезија

---

amputation

amputacija

ампутација

---

anaemia

anemija

анемија

anesthesiologist

anesteziolog

анестезиолог

antibiotics

antibiotici

антибиотици

anti-depressant

anti-depresivi

анти-депресиви

appointment

sastanak

састанак

arthritis

artritis

артритис

asthma

astma

астма

bacteria

bakterija

бактерија

bedsore

dekubitus

декубитус

---

biopsy

biopsija

биопсија

---

blood

krv

крв

---

blood count

krvna slika

крвна слика

---

blood donor

donator krvi

донатор крви

---

blood pressure

krvni pritisak

крвни притисак

---

blood test

test krvi

тест крви

---

bone

kost

кост

---

brace

pojas

појац

---

bruise

modrica

модрица

Caesarean section (C-section)

carski rez

царски рез

---

cancer

rak

рак

---

cardiopulmonary resuscitation (CPR)

kardiopulmonalna reanimacija

кардиопулмонална реанимација

---

case

slučaj

случај

---

cast

gips

гипс

---

chemotherapy

kemoterapija

кемотерапија

---

coroner

mrtvozornik

мртвозорник

critical

kritično

критично

crutches

štake

штаке

cyst

cista

циста

deficiency

nedostatak

недостатак

dehydrated

dehidriran

дехидриран

diabetes

dijabetes

дијабетес

diagnosis

dijagnoza

дијагноза

dietician

dijetetičar

дијететичар

disease

bolest

болест

doctor

doctor

доктор

emergency

hitno

хитно

emergency room (ER)

hitna služba

Хитна служба

exam

ispit

испит

fever

groznica

грозница

flu (influenza)

gripa

грипа

fracture

fraktura

фрактура

heart attack

srčani udar

срчани удар

hematologist

hematolog

хематолог

hives

osip

осип

hospital

bolnica

болница

illness

bolest

болест

imaging

snimak

снимак

immunization

Cijepljenje, vakcinacija

Цијепљење, вакцинација

infection

infekcija

инфекција

Intensive Care Unit (ICU)

jedinica intenzivne njege

јединица интензивне његе

IV

IV

ИВ

laboratory (lab)

laboratorij

лабораторij

life support

održavanje života

одржавање живота

mass

masa

маса

medical technician

medicinski tehničar

медицински техничар

neurosurgeon

neurokirurg

неурокирург

nurse

sestra

сестра

operating room (OR)

operaciona sala

операциона сала

operation

operacija

операција

ophthalmologist

oftamolog

офтамолог

orthopedic

ortopedski

ортопедски

pain

bol

бол

patient

pacijent

пацијент

pediatrician

pedijatar

педијатар

pharmacist

farmaceut

фармацеут

pharmacy

apoteka

апотека

physical Therapist

fizioterapeut

физиотерапеут

physician

doktor

доктор

poison

otrov

отров

prescription

recept

рецепт

psychiatrist

psihijatar

психијатар

radiologist

radiolog

радиолог

resident

specijalizant

специјализант

scan

skeniranje

скенирање

scrubs

pripravnici

приправници

shots

injekcije

инјекције

side effects

nuspojave

нуспојаве

specialist

specijalist

специјалист

stable

stabilno

стабилно

surgeon

hirurg

хирург

symptoms

simptomi

симптоми

therapy

terapija

терапија

treatment

liječenje

лијечење

vein

vena

вена

visiting hours

vrijeme posjeta

вријеме посјета

visitor

gost

гост

wheelchair

invalidska kolica

инвалидска колица

x-ray

rendgen

рендген

Related Verbs
Povezani glagoli
Повезани глаголи

to bring
donijeti
донијети

to cough
kašljati
кашљати

to examine
ispitati
испитати

to explain
objasniti
објаснити

to feel
osjećati
осјећати

to give
dati
дати

to hurt
povrijediti
повриједити

to prescribe

propisati

прописати

to scan

skenirati

скенирати

to take

uzeti

узети

to test

testirati

тестирати

to treat

liječiti

лијечити

to visit

posjetiti

посјетити

to wait

čekati

чекати

to x-ray

uraditi rengenski snimak

урадити ренгенски снимак

James was a happy, **healthy** ten year old boy who loved sports and riding his bike; but one day that all came to a halt. James had been complaining that his back was hurting. The **pain** was so bad one morning; he couldn't even get out of bed. His mom decided to take him to the **emergency room** to get **examined** by a **doctor**. The **nurses** were very friendly and their number one priority was making sure James was not in **pain** and could rest comfortably. The **doctor** decided to order an **x-ray** of his back. The **radiologist** read the report; he and the **ER doctor** agreed that James had an unknown **mass** on his spine. James was immediately admitted to the **hospital** for **blood tests**. The **blood tests** did not reveal the cause of the **mass,** so the **pediatrician** overseeing his **case** decided he needed some more extensive **imaging tests**, as well as a **biopsy.** James was nervous because so many **doctors** were coming to see him; an **orthopedic doctor**, a **neurosurgeon,** and a **hematologist.** The **nurses** did a good job at keeping his mind at ease. They brought him movies and video games to play to keep him busy. He had many **visitors**; friends and family members came to see him. He loved the visits with the **therapy** dogs the most; they were such comforting and sweet dogs. They had so many activities and fun for the **patients** at the children's **hospital**. James was a real trooper when they had to take **blood** and put his **IV** in his arm. James spent twelve days in the **hospital** before they finally **diagnosed** him with a **bone infection**. The **physical therapist** fit him with a back brace and he was **prescribed antibiotics**. After undergoing multiple **blood tests, image scans**, and a **biopsy**, James was ready to go home. He was not able to do the normal things other kids could do because of the damage to his spine, but he was so happy to be home with his family and on the mend from his terrible back **infection**. After several months of **treatment** and spinal **surgery** to straighten his back, James is now a strong, healthy, and happy boy. Through it all; the **treatments, tests, hospital** stays, and **therapy**, James has been an inspiration and hero to many who walked this journey with him.

Džejms je bio sretan, **zdrav** desetogodišnji dječak koji je volio sport i vožnju biciklom; ali jednog dana sve tose zaustavilo. Džejms se žalio da ga leđa bole. **Bol** je bila tako jaka jedno jutro da nije mogao ni ustati iz kreveta. Njegova mama je odlučila da ga odvede u **hitnu službu** kako bi ga **doktor** pregledao. **Medicinske sestre** su bile veoma ljubazne i njihov prioritet je bio da se pobrinuda Džejms ne bude u **bolovima** i da se može udobno odmoriti. **Doktor je** odlučio naručiti **rendgen snimak** njegovih leđa. **Radiolog** je pročitao izvještaj; on i **doktor iz hitne pomoći** su se složili da Džejms ima nepoznatu **masu** na kičmi. Džejms je odmah primljen u **bolnicu da uradi**nalaze **krvi. Krvni testovi** nisu otkrili uzrok **mase**, tako da je **pedijatar** nadzirao njegov slučaj i odlučio da je potrebno sprovesti opsežnije **snimanje tijela**, kao i **biopsiju**. Džejms je bio nervozan, jer je toliko doktora dolazilo da ga vidi; **ortopedi, neurohirurzi, hematolozi. Sestre** su uradile dobar posao i držale njegove misli zaokupljene. Donijeli su mu filmove i video igrice da igra kako bi ispunio vrijeme. Imao je mnogo **posjetitelja**; prijatelji i članovi porodice su došli da ga vide. Najviše je volio **posjete** sa **terapijskim** psima; oni su bili tako utješni i slatki psi. Imali su tako mnogo aktivnosti i zabave za **pacijente** u dječijoj bolnici. Džejms je bio veomahrabar kada bi mu morali vaditi **krv** i staviti **infuziju** u njegovu ruku. Džejms je proveo dvanaest dana u bolnici prije nego što mu je konačno **dijagnosticirana infekcija kostiju. Fizioterapeut** mu je namjestio **pojas za leđa**i propisani su mu

antibiotici. Nakon slijedećih **testova krvi**, **skenerskog snimanja** i **biopsije**, Džejms je bio spreman da ide kući. Nije mogaoda radi normalne stvari kao druga djeca zbog **oštećenja kičme**, ali je bio sretan da je kod kuće sa svojom porodicom i da **se oporavlja**od strašne leđne **infekcije**. Nakon nekoliko mjeseci **liječenja i operacije** da bi se ispravila kičma, Džejms je sada jak, zdrav i sretan dječak. Kroz sve to;**liječenje, testove, boravak u bolnicii terapije**, James je bio inspiracija i heroj mnogima koji su koračali kroz ovo putovanje sa njim.

Џејмс је био сретан, **здрав** десетогодишњи дјечак који је волио спорт и вожњу бициклом; али једног дана све тосе зауставило. Џејмс се жалио да га леђа боле. **Бол** је била тако јака једно јутро да није могао ни устати из кревета. Његова мама је одлучила да га одведе у **хитну службу** како би га **доктор** прегледао. **Медицинске сестре** су биле веома љубазне и њихов приоритет је био да осе побрину да Џејмс не буде у **боловима** и да се може удобно одморити. **Доктор** је одлучио наручити **рендген снимак** његових леђа. **Радиолог** је прочитао извјештај; он и **доктор из хитне помоћи** су се сложили да Џејмс има непознату **масу** на кичми. Џејмс је одмах примљен у **болницу** да уради **налазе крв**. **Крвни тестови** нису открили узрок **масе**, тако да је **педијатар** надзирао његов случај и одлучио да је потребно спровести опсежније **снимање тијела**, као и **биопсију**. Џејмс је био нервозан, јер је толико **доктора** долазило да га види; **ортопеди, неурохирурзи, хематолози. Сестре** су урадиле добар посао и држале његове мислизаокупљене. Донијели су му филмове и видео игрице да игра како би испунио вријеме. Имао је много **посјетитељ**а; пријатељи и чланови породице су дошли да га виде. Највише је волио **посјете** са

терапијским псима; они су били тако утјешни и слатки пси. Имали су тако много активности и забаве за **пацијенте** у дјечијој болници. Џејмс је био прави веома храбаркада би му морали вадити **крв** и ставити **инфузију** уњегову руку. Џејмс је провео дванаест дана у **болници** прије него што му је коначно **дијагностицирана инфекција костију**. **Физиотерапеут** му је намјестио **појас за леђа**и **прописани** цу му **антибиотици**. Након слиједећих **тестова крви, скенерског снимања и биопсије**, Џејмс је био спреман да иде кући. Није могаода ради нормалне ствари као друга дјеца због **оштећења** кичме, али је био сретан да је код куће са својом породицом и да се опоравља од страшне леђне **инфекције**. Након неколико мјесеци **лијечења и операције**да би се исправила кичма, Џејмс је сада јак, здрав и сретан дјечак. Кроз све то;**лијечење, тестове, боравак у болници**и **терапије**, Џејмс је био инспирација и херој многима који су корачали кроз ово путовање са њим.

18) Emergency
18) Hitan slučaj
18) Хитан случај

accident

nesreća

несрећа

---

aftershock

postraumatski

посттрауматски

---

ambulance

kola hitne pomoći

кола хитне помоћи

---

asthma attack

napad astme

напад астме

---

avalanche

lavina

лавина

---

blizzard

mećava

мећава

---

blood/ bleeding

krv/ krvarenje

крв/ крварење

broken bone

slomljena kost

сломљена кост

car accident

automobilska nesreća

аутомобилска несрећа

chest pain

bol u prsima

бол у прсима

choking

gušenje

гушење

coast guard

obalna straža

обална стража

crash

sudar

судар

diabetes

dijabetis

дијабетис

doctor
doctor
доктор

---

drought
suša
суша

---

drowning
utapanje
утапање

---

earthquake
zemljotres
земљотрес

---

emergency
hitno
хитно

---

emergency services
hitne službe
хитне службе

EMT (emergency medical technician)
EMT (medicinski tehničar hitne pomoći)
ЕМТ (медицински техничар хитне помоћи)

---

explosion
eksplozija
експлозија

---

fight
tuča
туча

fire
vatra
ватра

fire department
vatrogasna služba
ватрогасна служба

fire escape
požarne stepenice
пожарне степенице

firefighter
vatrogasac
ватрогасац

fire truck
vatrogasni kamion
ватрогасни камион

first aid
prva pomoć
прва помоћ

flood
poplava
поплава

fog

magla

магла

gun

pištolj

пиштољ

gunshot

pucanj

пуцањ

heart attack

srčani udar

срчани удар

heimlich maneuver

hajmlihov zahvat

хајмлихов захват

help

pomoć

помоћ

hospital

bolnica

болница

hurricane

uragan

ураган

injury

povreda

повреда

ladder

ljestve

љестве

lifeguard

spasilac

спасилац

life support

održavanje života

одржавање живота

lightening

munja

муња

lost

izgubljeno

изгубљено

mudslide

klizište

клизиште

natural disaster

elementarna nepogoda

елементарна непогода

nurse

medicinska sestra

медицинска сестра

officer

policajac

полицајац

paramedic

bolničar

болничар

poison

otrov

отров

police

policija

полиција

police car

policijsko auto

полицијско ауто

rescue

spašavanje

спашавање

robbery

pljačka

пљачка

shooting

pucnjava

пуцњава

stop

zaustavljanje

заустављање

storm

oluja

олуја

stroke

Moždani udar

Мождани удар

temperature

temperatura

температура

thief

lopov

лопов

tornado

tornado

торнадо

tsunami

cunami

цунами

unconscious

nesvjesno

несвјесно

---

weather emergency

vremenska nepogoda

временска непогода

Related Verbs
Povezani glagoli

Повезани глаголи

to bleed

krvariti

крварити

---

to break

slomiti

сломити

---

to breathe

disati

дисати

---

to burn

gorjeti

горјети

---

to call

zvati

звати

---

to crash

razbiti

разбити

to cut

rezati

резати

to escape

pobjeći

побјећи

to faint

onesvjestiti se

онесвјестити се

to fall

pasti

пасти

to help

pomoći

помоћи

to hurt

povrijediti

повриједити

to rescue

spasiti

спасити

to save

sačuvati

сачувати

to shoot

pucati

пуцати

to wheeze

hripati

хрипатикркљање

to wreck

uništiti

уништити

One of the most important things parents can teach their children is how to handle an **emergency**. You often hear stories on the news about a child who saved someone by making a wise decision in an **emergency**. What you don't hear are the stories when children made a poor decision. Unfortunately, many children would not know what to do in case of a real **emergency** such as a **fire**, a **flood**, or if a parent had a **heart attack**. We hope that our children are never put in these situations, but we want them to be prepared. In an **emergency**, such as a **tornado**, an **earthquake**, or other **natural disaster**, children might react in two very dangerous ways; one of which is the superhero reaction. In this case, children think they can "save the day" and play **rescue** worker. They might try to run into a burning building or swim out to save someone in a **flood.** Make sure your children know that there are people such as **firefighters, police officers**, and **EMTs** that are professionally trained to handle these situations. It may seem safe to "**help**", but the danger may not be obvious to a child. If they try to "**help**" in a dangerous situation, it may make the **emergency** worse! The best thing to do is call **emergency services** and they will tell you exactly what you can do to **help**. On the other hand, the opposite reaction can be just as dangerous. Some children will try to run and hide from scary situations. Even though you may be scared, try to remain calm, find a phone, and call for **help**. As I said earlier, children often play a big role in the **rescue** efforts during an **emergency**. Here are some practical tips to teach your children about **emergency** situations. 1) Take a deep breath, relax and look around for **help**. 2) Call for **help**; either by yelling or phone. If someone has an **injury** or ishurt, the **rescue** workers can be there fast. In a **life threatening** situation, the **emergency operator** can often walk you through step-by-step what to do. 3) Never hang up on the operator; they will need details about your location and the **emergency** situation. 4) Find a safe place to wait for help. Do not put yourself in danger while you wait for the professionals, it will only create a bigger **emergency**. The best way to handle an **emergency** is to prepare yourself for one. If you know what to do in different **emergencies**, you will be better equipped to handle them. Ask your parents to teach you the **fire escape** plan in your home or what to do in case someone is **injured** at home. Ask someone to show you how to call for help; make sure the phone numbers for the **fire department, police**, and **ambulance** service numbers are posted on your home phone. As you get older, you can even take a **first aid** class.

Remember, in all **emergencies**, remain calm and call for help and never put yourself in danger.

Jedna od najvažnijih stvari koje roditelji mogu naučiti svoju djecu jeste kako da postupesu **hitnim slučajevima**. Često na vijestima čujemo priče o djetetu koje je spasilo nekog donosećimudru odluku u **hitnom slučaju**. Ono što ne čujemo su priče kada djeca donose loše odluke. Nažalost mnoga djeca ne bi znala šta da urade u slučaju prave **nužde**, poput **požara**, **poplave** ili ako roditelj dobije **srčani udar**. Nadamo se da naša djeca nikada neće biti u ovakvim situacijama, ali želimo da budupripremljena. U **hitnom slučaju**, poput **tornada, zemljotresa** ili druge **prirodne katastrofe**, djeca mogu reagovati na dva veoma opasna načina; jedan od njih je reakcija super-heroja. U tom slučaju, djeca misle da mogu 'spasiti dan' i igradi se **spasitelja**. Mogu pokušati utrčati u zapaljenu zgradu ili zaplivati da bi spasili nekoga u **poplavi**. Pobrinite seda vaša djeca znaju da postoje ljudi poput **vatrogasaca, policajaca** i **medicinskih tehničara hitne pomoći** koji su stručno obučeniza ovakve situacije. Može se činiti sigurnim za '**pomoći**', ali opasnost možda nije očita djetetu. Ako pokušaju '**pomoći**' u opasnoj situaciji, **hitni slučaj** može postati još gori! Najbolja stvar je da nazovete **hitnu službu** i oni će vam tačno reći šta možete uraditi da **pomognete**. S druge strane, suprotna reakcija može također biti opasna. Neka djeca će pokušati pobjeći i sakriti se od zastrašujuće situacije. Iako ste možda prestrašeni, pokušajte ostati smireni, naći telefon i pozvati **pomoć**. Kao što sam rekao ranije, djeca često igraju veliku ulogu u **spašavanju** u **hitnim slučajevima**. Evo nekoliko praktičnih savjeta šta naučiti svoju djecu o **hitnim slučejevima**. 1) Duboko udahnite, opustite se i naokolo potražite **pomoć**; 2) Tražite**pomoć**; ili vikanjem ili telefonom. Ako neko ima **ozljedu** ili je povrijeđen, **spasioci** mogu biti tu brzo. U **životno opasnim situacijama, operator hitne pomoći** često može da vam pokaže korak-po-korak šta da uradite; 3) Nikada nemojte spuštati slušalicu operatoru; oni moraju imati detalje o vašoj lokaciji i **hitnom slučaju**; 4) Nađite sigurno mjesto gdje ćete sačekati pomoć. Nemojte se izlagati opasnosti dok čekate profesionalce, to će samo stvoriti još veću **hitnost**. Najbolji način da se nosite sa **hitnim slučajem** je da se pripremite za jedan takav. Ako znate šta raditi u različitim **hitnim slučajevima**, biti ćete bolje pripremljeni dase nosite sa njima. Pitajte roditelje da vas nauče **planu za bijeg od požara** u tvom domu ili šta uraditi ako je neko **povrijeđen** kod kuće. Pitajte nekoga da vam pokaže kako nazvati pomoć; pobrinite seda su telefonski brojevi **vatrogasaca, policije i hitne službe** upisani u kućnom telefonu. Kada budete stariji, možete čak i pohađati kurs**prve pomoći**. Zapamtite, u svim **hitnim slučajevima**, ostanite mirni i pozovite pomoć i nikad se ne izlažite opasnosti.

Једна од најважнијих ствари које родитељи могу научити своју дјецу јесте како да се носе у **хитним случајевима**. Често на вијестима чујемо приче о дјетету које је спасило неког доносећи мудру одлуку у **хитном случају**. Оно што не чујемо су приче када дјеца доносе лоше одлуке. Нажалост многа дјеца не би знала шта да ураде у случају праве **нужде**, попут **пожара, поплаве** или ако родитељ добије **срчани удар**. Надамо се да наша дјеца никада неће бити у оваквим ситуцијама, али желимо да буду припремљени. **У хитном случају**, попут **торнада, земљотреса** или друге **природне катастрофе**, дјеца могу реаговати на два веома опасна начина; један од њих је реакција супер-херој. У том случају, дјеца мисле да могу 'спасити дан' и игради се **спаситеља**. Могу покушати утрчати у запаљену зграду или запливати да би спасили некога у **поплави**. Побрините седа ваша дјеца знају да постоје људи попут **ватрогасаца, полицајаца и медицинских техничара хитне помоћи** који су стручно обученида за овакве ситуације. Може се чинити сигурним за '**помоћи**', али опасност можда није очита дијетету. Ако покушају '**помоћи**' у опасној ситуацији, **хитни случај** може постати још гори! Најбоља ствар је да назовете **хитну службу** и они ће вам тачно рећи шта можете урадити да **помогнете.**С друге стране, супротна реакција може такођер бити опасна. Нека дјеца ће покушати побјећи и сакрити се од застрашујуће ситуације. Иако сте можда престрашени, покушајте остати смирени, наћи телефон и позвати **помоћ**. Као што сам рекао раније, дјеца често играју велику улогу у **спашавању** у **хитним случајевима**. Ево неколико практичних савјета штанаучити своју дјецу о **хитним случејевима**. 1) Дубоко уддахните, опустите се и наоколо потражите **помоћ**; 2) Тражитепомоћ; или викањемили телефоном. Ако неко има **озљеду** или је повријеђен, **спасиоци** могу бити ту брзо. У **животно опасним ситуацијама, оператор хитне помоћи** често може да вам покаже корак-по-корак шта да урадите; 3) Никада немојте спуштати слушалицу оператору; они морају имати детаље о вашој локацији и **хитном случају**; 4) Нађите сигурно мјесто гдје ћете сачекати помоћ. Немојте се излагати опасности док чекате професионалце, то ће само створити још већу **хитност**. Најбољи начин да се носите са **хитним случајем** је да се припремите за један такав. Ако знате шта радити у различитим **хитним случајевима**, бит ћете боље припремљенидасе носите са њима. Питајте родитеље да васнауче **плану за бијег од пожара** у вашемдому или шта урадити ако је неко **повријеђен** код куће. Питајте некога да вам покаже како назвати помоћ; побрините седа су телефонски бројеви **ватрогасаца, полиције и хитне службе** уписани у кућном телефону. Када будете старији, можете чак и похађати курс**прве помоћи**. Запамтите, у свим **хитним случајевима**, останите мирни и позовите помоћ и никад се не излажите опасности.

Made in the
USA
Monee, IL

15072041R00210